MONEY NUMBER ONE

By
Neil Hutchison

Copyright © Neil Hutchison, 2006
First Edition Published 2006

Published by
DCO Books
Proglen Trading Co., Ltd.
Bangkok Thailand
http://ebooks.dco.co.th

ISBN 978-1500669270

All Rights Reserved

Neil Hutchison

Email: hutcho_ph@yahoo.com
Website: www.moneynumberone.net

Disclaimer

Since the end of the world did not occur on 21 December 2012 as we all expected, this revised 2013 Edition of *Money Number One* is now available. This book is the same as earlier editions except it has been updated to reflect the many changes which have occurred in Pattaya over the past twelve months. As with all previous editions, the author shirks all responsibility for the content and offers the following warning:

This book is for entertainment only and was written in the spirit of fun. No disrespect or offence to any individual or group of people is intended or implied. These pages contain generalizations, anecdotes and references to personal experiences, observations and opinions. Stories relating to the author's personal experiences are as accurate as his alcohol-affected memory will allow.

Absolutely no effort has been made to authenticate stories passed on by third parties. Stories told through word of mouth tend to change somewhat each time they are related, but they are included because in the opinion of the author, editor and publisher, each one reflects a plausible scenario. Any similarity or resemblance to any person alive or dead is their problem.

Tips and advice are offered with the best of intentions but if you come to Thailand for a holiday, follow any or all the suggestions offered and still screw up, it's your problem.

The prices referred to throughout this book are quoted in Thai *baht*. Although due care has been taken, they are approximations and should only be used as a guide.

Contents

Chapter 1 Preface 7
 2 Introduction 8
 3 Magnificent Pattaya 14
   When to Come
   Songkran
   How to Get Here
   Places to Stay
   Personal Safety
   Travelling About
   Money
   Food
   Drugs
   STDs and AIDS
   Health & Medical
   Returning to the Airport
 4 People of Many Faces 44
   Nineteen Lessons about the Locals
 5 Adult Fun & Entertainment .. 64
   Go-Go Bars
   Indoor Recreation Lounges
   Beer Bars
   The Games People Play
   Gambling
   Massages
   Other Entertainment
 6 The Hostesses 82
   Life of a Pattaya Bar Hostess
   Freelancers
   Exotic Language of the Bars
   Bar Hostess v *Farang*
   Bar Speak

7	General Observations	110

Tips for saving money and
not looking stupid.

8	The *Farang*	120

The Butterfly
The Cheap Charlie

9	*Farang* in Love	130

Early Danger Signs
Financial Support
The Absent Boyfriend
Going on 'Holiday'
Correspondence

10	Her Family	154

Visiting Her Family
When Her Relatives Visit You

11	Marriage-minded	164

Advice for those men
with marriage on their mind

12	*Farang* Businessmen	172

Advice for those men
wishing to start a business venture

13	Conclusion	180

Including some reader's comments

MONEY NUMBER ONE

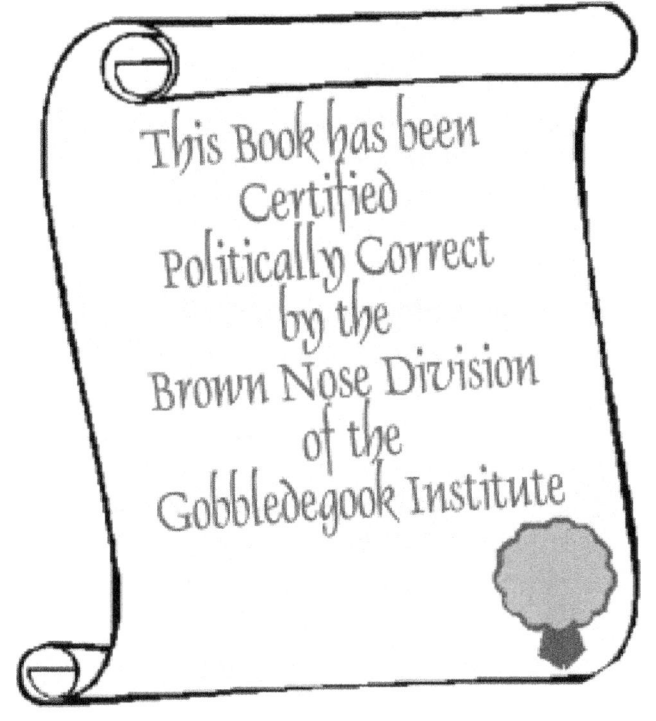

NEIL HUTCHISON

Preface

"In any country where talent and virtue produce no advancement, money will be the national god. Its inhabitants will either have to possess money or make others believe that they do. Wealth will be the highest virtue, poverty the greatest vice. Those who have money will display it in every imaginable way. If their ostentation does not exceed their fortune, all will be well. But if their ostentation does exceed their fortune they will ruin themselves. In such a country, the greatest fortunes will vanish in the twinkling of an eye. Those who don't have money will ruin themselves with vain efforts to conceal their poverty. That is one kind of affluence: the outward sign of wealth for a small number, the mask of poverty for the majority, and a source of corruption for all."

Denis Diderot (1713-84), French philosopher.
written in 1774 for Catherine the Great of Russia.

MONEY NUMBER ONE

1
Introduction

On Christmas Eve 2001, the first edition of *Money Number One,* subtitled 'The Single Man's Survival Guide to Pattaya', was released in Pattaya. It was a book like none other before it. The author had obviously conducted extensive and expensive research in his attempt to produce an informative and humorous traveller's guide. Offering constructive advice in a light-hearted and anecdotal manner, it attempted to explain many of the traps which lie waiting for men who arrive in Pattaya to discover a thirst is mandatory, a fat wallet is obligatory and morality is listed as an optional extra. It received very kind reviews from English language press in Thailand (*Bangkok Post*; *Pattaya Today*; *Pattaya Mail*) and very supportive praise from a young Thai female reviewer in *Ying Thai* magazine, a popular monthly women's magazine.

In his *Bangkok Post* review of *Money Number One*, Bernard Trink wrote, "Hutchison might have pointed out that much of what he suggests unique to Pattaya applies to Bangkok as well." Mr Trink's view is correct and what applies in Pattaya bars also applies to other adult entertainment areas throughout Asia. Investigating them all would require time and money so, with no evidence to the contrary, if you are reading this in a bar in Bangkok, Phuket, Chiang Mai, Phnom Penh, Manila or Angeles City, you can, relative to the general advice offered, substitute the name of your location for Pattaya. Furthermore, reliable sources suggest that gay men (nothing wrong with that) may substitute the masculine equivalent of the gender-specific terms used throughout this book and the story is virtually the same thing.

NEIL HUTCHISON

I asked a Pattaya Bar Hostess if it was indeed true that money is number one. Her response of, "Not true. For me, farang number one," sent me into deep shock until she restored my faith by smiling and adding, "because they give me money."

The updated second edition called *Money Still Number One* was published in May 2004 and a year later a full-page article appeared in the Thai daily newspaper, *Matichon*, decrying the book as denegrating Thai womanhood. A few Pattaya Bar Hostesses apparently believed the book was teaching foreigners what they did not want them to know; divulging too many secrets. One comment was that Pattaya's Bar Hostesses were 'crying' because *Money Still Number One* was responsible for 'reducing their income'.

The book was voluntarily withdrawn from sale and the author forced to flee the country and move to Tibet, where he promised to devote whatever remained of his miserable life to meditation, self-flagellation and the search for inner peace.

After close scrutiny of all Neil Hutchison's books by the Thai Ministry of Culture, it found no case to answer. It transpired that this was just a vindictive attack by one unscrupulous individual. Pattaya streets were not filled with angry Bar Hostesses bearing torches and carrying buckets of tar and feathers, seeking out the author of the book they mistakenly believed portrayed them as being less than the honest, virtuous maidens they perceive themselves to be. Some people have no sense of humour.

The third edition, reverting to the original name *Money Number One*, came out in July 2006 after being re-edited, revised and updated by a brown-nosing pommie from Chelsea, London, with the poncy name Aloysius Bartholemew Thistlewaite. He retained all the good, honest and informative advice while redrafting the anecdotes and opinions in a politically correct way so the words could not be taken out of context. The result was a 'Politically Correct' version, guaranteed to make it impossible for even the most insecure, xenophobic, self-centred, thin-skinned, snivelling whinger to take offence. The result can be likened to an episode of that entertaining and educational television series, *Kung Fu*, in which the old Chinese Master was teaching his disciple, the not very Asian-looking David Carradine:

"Remember, Grasshopper, any foolish man can learn from reading lines of prose. A wise man learns more by reading between them."

MONEY NUMBER ONE

The *Special 2012 Doomsday Edition* brought readers up to date with the changing Pattaya scene but was not available in bookshops as a hard copy. Likewise, this *2013 'Lucky for Some' Edition* is also only available in electronic form.

It is impossible for any book to cover every contingency, but the e-mails received from readers confirm what *Money Number One* does cover is right on the mark.

"I wish I had read this book before I first set foot in Thailand."

This was the most common response and an indication that the person would have had a much better time in Thailand had he been given more reliable information from the outset. The newly arrived male visitor to dazzling Pattaya finds himself in a Disneyland for adults, a place unlike anywhere else on this planet. He sees the neon Pattaya which greets the holidaymaker, wears him down, chews him up then spits him out ten days later. Many foreign visitors make just about every mistake there is to make and fall for every sweet mouth. Even after several trips and in spite of all the advice, they are still paying vet bills for sick buffalo, still paying for new roofs for distant houses, still buying motorcycles for unseen relatives and still getting dumped by the love of their life once their money runs out. Of course, if they knew then what they know now, things would have been different. Perhaps.

Tourists are taken advantage of in every country. Some object to it strongly while others consider it the price they pay for a lack of local knowledge. Whichever way you look at it, anyone who is cheated, ripped off or falls in love with a local resident who subsequently empties his wallet or bank account will return home to report that holiday destination was a terrible place and advise friends against going. That is in spite of how idyllic it might have otherwise been.

If, however, either before arriving or while there, he reads an honest book explaining how to behave, how to be careful and use common sense, some of the pitfalls associated with being a stranger in a foreign land can be avoided. Result: He has a great time and reports it is a wonderful place to visit.

"I'm going to take this book home to show my friends, because they don't believe me when I tell them about Pattaya."

NEIL HUTCHISON

To anyone who has never been here, Pattaya is almost impossible to describe. With truth and logic the early casualties, the reality is that here, single foreign men are no longer the predator but the quarry, no longer the hunter but the hunted. Recounting Pattaya exploits to the uninitiated back home loses its thrill when continually met with looks of disbelief.

"There is one place in Thailand I hate more than anywhere else on the planet - the departure lounge at Bangkok airport."

If e-mails are anything to go by, that sentiment is shared by thousands of men, with one guy actually confessing he was in tears as he boarded the plane home. *Suvarnabhumi* airport departure lounge must be the most depressing place in the world. The reason is simple. Pattaya is such a fun and exciting town it can be addictive - more addictive than nicotine or alcohol.

Sitting in the departure lounge, the withdrawal symptoms can be acute once the visitor realizes there is no turning back - he must get on the plane and he must go home. But 'reality' and the 'real world' will never be the same again. Suddenly, the weather back home seems exceptionally cold, wet and miserable. Suddenly, the girl in the office or the local pub, the one who he has been trying to chat up for the last six months, is not as pretty as he previously thought.

So why not simply enjoy the place and forget about trying to understand it? Because the Pattaya addiction can get you down if you let it. It can defeat you if you let it and, in the final analysis, it can break you if you let it. Knowledge is power and the more you understand how and why something works, the more chance you have of working with it and enjoying it.

Many foreign men come to Thailand, make fools of themselves, fall in love with a charming local lady and marry after a two-week whirlwind romance. The Self-Appointed Foreign Defenders of the Realm, (S.A.F.D.R.), preach that being married to a Thai is the ultimate honour and such liaisons have no less chance of success than Western marriages. Further, if the union does break down, it is almost exclusively due to a lack of understanding exhibited by the Western spouse of the cultural superiority of his faultless Thai partner. True or not, most love-struck Western men would benefit from more knowledge before taking the plunge. Learn first, fall in love later.

MONEY NUMBER ONE

Someone once said, "If you could give the person most responsible for your problems a big kick up the arse, you wouldn't be able to sit down for a month."

If, after reading *Money Number One*, you are even more firmly committed to carving out a niche for youself in this amazing place called Thailand, there are three other books which are highly recommended reading. The novel *Bangkok 8* by John Burdett, published by Corgi Books, is set in Bangkok and is supposed to be totally fictional. That is probably the case as far as the plot goes but, as a glimpse into the underworld and seedy subculture of Thailand, the author shows remarkable insight. Even if not into the detective-murder-mystery genre, some of the dialogue and observations will help foreign readers appreciate a little of the Thai view of their world.

Thailand Fever by Chris Pirazzi and Vitida Vasant, published by Paiboon Publishing, is a guide for foreigners finding themselves in a relationship with a Thai. Just as *Money Number One* is a 'must read' for foreign men coming to Thailand NOT to see the temples, *Thailand Fever* is a 'must read' for any Western male contemplating entering a romantic relationship with a Thai lady. In both English and Thai, it contains explanations of her 'Thai ways' so you won't be left scratching your head at some of her behaviour. She can learn about you as well because, if there is something you feel needs explaining, you can point out the corresponding paragraph in Thai for her.

The novel *Private Dancer* by Stephen Leather is a chilling story about a mutually destructive relationship between a foreigner and a beautiful Bangkok Go Go dancer. It tends to be very cynical but makes valuable reading because it probably represents the worst case scenario. (It would be difficult to imagine a more tragic tale.) The author does a great job of exposing the difference between the Thai idea of 'love' and the Western concept of 'love', while showing just how blinded a foreign man in love can be to truth and reality.

Writing a book like *Money Number One* is not easy. It involves hours upon hours of painstaking research; sitting in bars, dives and seedy rooms night after night; forced to speak with some of the most beautiful women in the world. It means fighting a losing battle against alcoholism to the extent of writing for hours before realizing you've been using the wrong end of the pencil. It means developing theories about places and people then having to test them out to make sure the strategy works more than just the one time. Consequently, it means making mistakes, faux pas, goofs and blunders because you don't follow your own advice and instincts. It means being a stupid *farang*.

Appreciation goes to those expats and holidaymakers who bravely bared their souls to pass on advice and share anecdotes from their often embarrassing experiences for inclusion in these pages. There is no such person as an 'expert' on Thailand because here, experience is the only teacher and the class lasts a lifetime. Nevertheless, the learning process certainly makes life interesting. So pull up a bar stool, order yourself a drink and pay attention.

> *"Let us have wine and women, mirth and laughter,*
> *Sermons and soda-water the day after."*
> Lord Byron (1788–1824), English poet.

3
Magnificent Pattaya

According to 2010 statistics, Pattaya/Banglamung is home to some 150,000 permanent Thai residents, probably the same number of unregistered residents and, at any one time, up to 20,000 foreign expats. It is also home to 100,000 motor vehicles and about 300,000 motorcycles, all of which seem to be on the road at the same time. Just under two hours drive from Bangkok, it is situated on a bay, is compact and has everything a foreign tourist could possibly want. And it is booming, with new hotels, apartment blocks and businesses springing up at a remarkable pace. Wherever you may travel in the world, there is nowhere like Pattaya. Geographically, it may be located in Thailand, but it is not typical of Thailand. Outwardly, it may have the appearance of being European or American, but it is not. Pattaya is a confluence of cultures, both East and West, Thai and non-Thai. It would be a mistake for visitors to judge the place by its appearance and an even greater error to judge the Thai people by what you see or hear during a short holiday in Pattaya.

Improving Pattaya's international image by promoting the resort as a family destination has not been a waste of time. Millions of 'budget' and 'high-class' tourists arrive with their friends or families for a wholesome vacation. The majority of families, couples and unattached foreign women have a very enjoyable time. Many opt for accommodation in the quieter areas of Jomtien (south of Pattaya) or Naklua (north of Pattaya) but even those who stay in the centre of town could spend a week or more without exposure to the type of activities for which Pattaya is more famous. Even if they do interact with the bars, the meritorious Hostesses of Pattaya's adult entertainment areas treat foreign women incredibly well and, as for children, Thai girls are crazy about them. The hostesses will play with them, keep them amused, dote over them and generally take better care of them than professional baby-sitters. The kids have a great time.

There are also visitors, not exclusively male, who come to partake in the style of entertainment and partying at which Pattaya excels. Those who come here specifically for the nightlife find themselves with plenty to occupy their time. Once the sun sets, a full spectrum of delights awaits them, adapted to suit everyone from the shy first-timer to the guy who believes 'Sleazy' was not just the name of the eighth dwarf.

Because of this, and in spite of its well-earned popularity, some foreign writers have had a field day 'Pattaya Bashing', describing it as a brothel, dangerous or a haven for foreign paedophiles, drug addicts and criminals. This garbage is written by journalistic hacks who spend a few days here and sensationalize their copy in order to sell newspapers. The people who live here and frequent visitors know that writing the truth would sell more plane tickets than newspapers.

For the foreigner [*farang*], Pattaya can be a cheap holiday or an expensive one. Hotel rates are generally cheaper than in Bangkok and Phuket, while restaurants are also less expensive. Tourists who come here for ten days with a seemingly endless supply of cash and a pressing desire to throw it all away as quickly as possible will have the time of their lives. With no shortage of people eager to accept their money, when you ask the locals later what they thought of the free-spending foreigner, some politely suggest he could have been a little more careful with his financial disbursements. In the local vernacular that comes out as "Stupid *farang*".

When to Come

Apart from the extraordinarly heavy monsoon of 2011 which flooded northern Thailand and Bangkok (but not Pattaya), the weather is usually perfect in Thailand. Visitors used to colder climates may be forgiven for assuming that between April and October it is very hot and wet. The truth is the warm glow covering the perfect landscape is occasionally broken by gentle raindrops falling to earth like petals to enrich the fertile soil. May to

MONEY NUMBER ONE

November is called the 'low season' because there are fewer tourists about and business is not as active. Airfares to Thailand are usually lower, the already very affordable accommodation is plentiful and room rates are even cheaper.

From December to April, called the 'high season', it is pleasantly hot and dry although December can be refreshingly cool, especially during the Christmas-New Year period. There are many more tourist arrivals, escaping freezing conditions in their home countries, and hotels are often heavily booked. If you plan to be here during this time, ensure you book a room in advance and reconfirm your booking just before leaving home. Veteran travellers are aware that in every country in the world, some hotel managers have the annoying habit of double-booking or forgetting.

For most single men, especially those whose passions extend no further than nocturnal activities, any time is a good time to come to Pattaya. The population of charming hostesses expands and contracts in proportion to the number of tourists so many men prefer to be in Pattaya during the low season when it is not so crowded. Bars and places of entertainment often discount their prices to attract the fewer customers and even the breathtaking hostesses are vulnerable to a bit of bargaining.

> **_TIP_**
> *On your first trip to Pattaya it is wise to pre-book a room even if only for your first two days. You will at least be assured of a bed while you check out other places to stay for the rest of your trip. If the hotel is to your liking, it is easy to extend your booking. Changing hotels, though, is not a bad idea as you will find out in a later chapter.*

Songkran

Special mention must be made of the annual *Songkran* festival which, in Pattaya, is held from the 12th to the 19th of April. *Songkran* is a Thai word meaning 'move' or 'change place' and is used to describe the day when the sun shifts its position in the zodiac. Often called the 'water festival', *Songkran* is supposed to be a gentle and solemn Thai ceremony heralding in the wet season and the Thai New Year in accordance with the Buddhist calendar. Many Thais believe water will wash away bad luck and cleanse them of their sins, prompting one local wit to observe: "The fact that Pattaya's entire Thai population spends a whole week and uses millions of litres of water to wash away its collective sins maybe gives an indication of what the natives think of themselves and may serve to put the city in perspective."

Songkran, Pattaya style, is seven days of sheer madness and the world's biggest water fight. Many smarter residents take advantage of this time to take their annual vacation in another country. For people who stay, it means being continually wet for seven days. Not just damp - totally soaking, dripping wet. It is fantastic fun but you must have a strong sense of humour and a strong tolerance for water. It is also a time to take extra care on the roads. Throughout Thailand there are more than 500 deaths and over 34,000 injuries in vehicle accidents during the *Songkran* celebration. These accidents are attributed to a combination of alcohol consumption and the throwing of water. Around 80% of the accidents involve motorcycles, so take the hint. If you come to Pattaya for *Songkran*, do everyone a favour and bring some common sense with you. Do not throw or fire a blast of water at anyone riding a motorcycle. The water can blind them for a few seconds and anything can happen.

The last day of the Pattaya festival, the 19th, is the craziest day of all and has to be seen to be believed. Most of the local Thai population participate and the fun begins early morning. Traffic comes to a standstill as the streets become awash with water and white powder. This is the *only* day it is permissible to wet a uniformed police officer, but please leave that to the Thais. It would be a great risk for a foreigner to attract the attention or angst of any policeman by dousing him with water.

Prior to *Songkran* 2002, an interesting article appeared in the *Bangkok Post* declaring that, "Police have been banned from using water guns to shoot at passers-by during the *Songkran* celebration." Apparently, there were concerns a police officer might get confused and use his real firearm by mistake. It would be extremely worrying to think that the well-trained, well-disciplined, elite Royal Thai Police do not have the capacity to differentiate between a large, pink, plastic, 'Star Wars' type water cannon and a small, heavy, metallic side-arm. In order to curb the mayhem, the *Pattaya Mail* reported, "Pattaya police issued a strong warning to all residents and tourists celebrating the *Songkran* festival that anyone found using ice, dangerous items like home-made water guns from PVC pipes, dirty water, or powder of any kind will be fined 2,000 *baht*. The warning stated that drunk and disorderly behaviour and any form of sexual harassment will also face strong penalties and a hefty fine. Police ask that everyone respect the traditional values of *Songkran* and Thai culture."

The way to survive *Songkran* is to be prepared and take extra care on the streets. Do not drive your car or motorbike anywhere. Do not plan on catching *baht* buses or motorcycle taxis either. They make perfect targets and, in any case, it is faster to walk. Unless you plan to join in the fun, go out only when necessary and when you do go out, dress in light, casual, quick drying clothing and don't wear your best shoes. Expect to get a total soaking, so when you are hit with water don't get upset or angry. Don't wear a wristwatch unless it is waterproof to sixty metres. Better still, don't wear a watch. Similarly, leave the mobile phone and non-waterproof camera at home. Put your cash and anything else you desperately need to take with you into re-sealable watertight plastic bags and, if you are a smoker, do the same with your cigarettes and lighter. In fact, use several plastic bags as the water always seems to penetrate the outer one.

> *On a serious note, I have made it a rule only to spray water over Bar Hostesses, those street kids who for most of the year annoy me by trying to sell me chewing gum or cigarette lighters, people in wheelchairs and people taking anti-diarrhoea medication. As you can see, my strategy is to pick on those who are least able to fight back.*

How to Get Here

On the 28th September 2006, *Suvarnabhumi* Airport situated some 30 kilometres to the southeast of central Bangkok and only a 90-minute drive from Pattaya, opened with little fanfare after four and a half years of construction. Pronounced 'soo-warn-a-poom', the name means 'Golden Peninsula' or 'Golden Land', a traditional name for the Burma-Thailand-Cambodia-Laos region.

Built to handle 45 million passengers per year, *Suvarnabhumi* was found lacking so in 2007 the government made the sensible decision to reopen *Don Muang* Airport which had been servicing only charter flights since its closure. Initially it was proposed that *Don Muang* be used primarily for domestic flights but the problems with *Suvarnabhumi* were deemed so severe that the old airport opened for budget international carriers as well. Air Asia, Nok Air (domestic flights) and One-Two-Go (domestic flights) are three airlines which currently operate from *Don Muang*. In case other airlines join them, passengers are advised to check the airport code on the ticket: BKK is *Suvarnabhumi* and DMK is *Don Muang*.

Both airports can be confusing and intimidating at first, but if you use common sense, there is nothing to be overly concerned about. What follows is a step-by-step guide for inexperienced visitors.

NEIL HUTCHISON

1. Getting off the Plane.

This sounds very simple but you would be surprised at the number of people who incur avoidable problems. Before landing, the airline crew should have given you a Thai arrival/departure card, commonly called a 'TM' card, to fill out. If not, ask for one. Immediately complete and sign BOTH the 'Arrival' and 'Departure' sections of the card, then turn it over and fill in the questionnaire on the back of the 'Arrival' section. (For the question about your annual income, I suggest you pick any box other than '0'.)

Once you have landed, before leaving the aircraft, make sure you have your Boarding Pass stub with you. Although it may have changed recently, Thai Immigration used to require that you show your Boarding Pass at Passport Control. It is better to be safe than sorry because, if you leave it on the plane it is a long walk back to retrieve it.

2. Airport Protocol.

Whichever airport you arrive at, once off the plane and onto the concourse, just follow the crowd to the Passport Control counters. There are hundreds of these so stand in line at the one or two actually open. Tourists from many countries do not require a Visa to Thailand and are granted a 30-day Tourist entry stamp on arrival. If you are unsure whether this applies to your nationality, ask the travel agent BEFORE you leave home. In any case, they probably won't issue you the plane ticket unless you possess the necessary visa.

At the Immigration desk, hand over your passport, completed TM Card and Boarding Pass. People travelling on Tourist Visas or seeking a 30-day Tourist entry stamp on arrival are required to have an outbound or return ticket. You may be asked to show this as well. Smile, don't chat, and be very polite – "Yes, sir"; "No, sir"; "Thank you, sir." Many people don't realize that gaining entry to a foreign country is not a right but a privilege. Entry can be refused or revoked at any time for any reason and the Immigration Officer with the rubber stamp wields enormous power. Should he or she be having a 'bad hair day' aggravated by your insolence, it could make your initiation to Thailand extremely unpleasant.

Once through Immigration, for those with checked-in luggage to collect, look for the monitor displaying the carousel number corresponding to your flight. Once all your possessions are in hand, proceed through the 'Customs' doorway. Now the real fun begins.

MONEY NUMBER ONE

At *Suvarnabhumi* Airport, most international visitors will leave the Customs area through Exit B leading into the main Arrivals Hall. At *Don Muang*, it will be Terminal 1. If you do not already have some local currency on you, now is a good time to get some. The Thai currency unit is called the *baht* (pronounced as in Bart Simpson) and the notes come in denominations of 1,000 (highest); 500; 100; 50 (not very common); and 20. Within both airport complexes, the 24-hour ATM's have instructions in both Thai and English and dispense 1,000 *baht* notes, 500 *baht* notes and 100 *baht* notes up to a maximum of 20 notes per transaction.

For people exchanging cash or traveller's cheques, the rates do not vary between the Currency Exchanges so don't bother shopping around. Ask for some smaller denominations – 100's and 20's. At this point, most tourists would not require more than 5,000 *baht* in cash for transport and/or a hotel room deposit.

For anyone feeling hungry or with some time to kill, both airports have many places to eat. At *Don Muang*, just follow the signs to any of the fast food restaurants. At *Suvarnabhumi* Airport, the cheapest is Magic Food Point on the ground level next to Gate 8. It is a typical Thai food court where you purchase coupons. The many food offerings start from 25 *baht*. Outside is a Family Mart convenience store.

3.   Getting to Pattaya.
Pattaya-bound tourists travelling direct from the airports have several transport options depending on how many people in their group, how much luggage they brought and the arrival time. Please note all fares quoted were correct at the time of writing but may have since increased.

Limousine
If money is no object or you have others to share the cost, the elite way to travel is by the Thai Airways Limousine Service. From either airport, the comfortable trip will cost around 4,000 *baht* which includes any motorway tolls. Confirm these details before you book.

Taxi
A cheaper but equally quick option is to go by taxi. The new Airport Authority does not appear to allow private operators to tout for business, so people wishing to take a taxi should head down one level from the 'Arrivals' floor and walk outside to one of the three Service Desks and army of waiting vehicles. For transport to within Bangkok and Greater Bangkok, the fare is charged as shown on the meter plus any tolls plus a 50

baht Airport Service Charge. The fare to Pattaya is set by the Airport Authority at 1,300 *baht* which includes all tolls and charges. Check just to make sure. Depending on traffic, the trip from *Suvarnabhumi* to Central Pattaya should take around 90 minutes.

From *Don Muang* Airport, taxis with or without meters will be happy to take you to Pattaya. A reasonable fare is 1,600 *baht* which may or may not include up to three motorway tolls totalling about 135 *baht*. Check and negotiate beforehand and ask the driver if it is the same vehicle that will be taking you all the way to Pattaya. It is common practice for the car/taxi waiting at the airport to be only the delivery vehicle to take you to their office where you transfer to another car/taxi which takes you the rest of the way. No real problem, just scary the first time. Unless you have a mountain of luggage, do not put it in the trunk of the car. Keep it on the seat beside you and never leave it unattended. The trip should take around two and a half hours.

Bus

Large, yellow, air-conditioned buses (Route 389) go to Pattaya direct from *Suvarnabhumi* airport. They don't actually go into Pattaya city but travel along *Sukhumvit* Road stopping at each major intersection before terminating at Jomtien Bus Station on *Chaiyaphruek* Road at the far southern end of Jomtien Beach. The cost is 106 *baht* but there are only four per day, departing at 9:00am, 1:00pm, 5:00pm and 8:00pm from the Public Transportation Center. To get to that, catch one of the free Shuttle Buses which are supposed to leave every 20 minutes.

Alternatively, Bell Travel Service operates buses to Pattaya departing from the Arrivals Hall on the hour every two hours between 8:00am and 6:00pm. These terminate at the bus station in Pattaya North Road and the trip should take around ninety minutes.

Every 30 minutes from 5:00am until midnight, the AE3 bus departs from in front of the Passenger Terminal Complex and travels to *Soi Nana* in Bangkok along *Sukhumvit* Road, stopping at the Eastern Bus Terminal at Ekamai for a fare of 150 *baht*. From there, air-conditioned buses leave for Pattaya every thirty minutes between 5:00am and 10:00pm. The current fare is 120 *baht*. Anyone preferring to travel to Ekamai by taxi, the fare from the airport is approximately 150 *baht* plus the 50 *baht* airport surcharge.

From *Don Muang* airport, Pattaya-direct buses depart at 9:00am, 12:00 noon and 7:00pm for a fare of 200 *baht*. Every thirty minutes between 5:00am and 7:00pm buses leave for Pattaya from the Northern Bus Terminal at Morchit. The taxi fare to Morchit is around 120 *baht* plus the 50 *baht*

MONEY NUMBER ONE

airport surcharge. An airport Shuttle Bus will transport you to Morchit BTS (Skytrain) and Chatuchak Park MRT stations for 30 *baht* and from there it is easy to get to either Ekamai or Morchit bus terminals.

The bus services from Morchit and Ekamai terminate at the bus station in Pattaya North Road. To get to your hotel, catch one of the pick-ups, commonly called '*Baht* Buses', which wait at the bus station and travel a set route for 20 *baht* per person. If your hotel is located on Beach or Second Roads, this is a good option. Simply press the buzzer when you want to get out. If you don't have a clue where your hotel is located, ask one of the drivers who will take you directly for a fare starting at 40 *baht* per person. It depends how far the hotel is from the bus station, but the maximum fare for one-way group transfer from North Pattaya to anywhere else in the greater Pattaya area is 120 *baht*. That is for a maximum of five people, NOT each!

Train

The new Airport Rail Link between *Suvarnabhumi* and Bangkok is now operational and the Express Service to the City Terminal at *Makkasan* takes 20 minutes for a fare of 150 *baht*. The service supposedly operates every 15 minutes between 6:00am and 11:30pm.

Please be warned that the Airport Rail Link has had teething problems and officials have been bombarded with complaints of shoddy service; the terminals at the stations being badly signposted; lack of escalators and no provision of trolleys for passengers with heavy bags. Other complaints include the lack of a car park and no facilities linking the stations to public transport. If any of that worries you, it might be an idea to give the speedy train a miss for now.

Believe it or not, there is a train service to Pattaya from Bangkok's Central *Hualampong* Station, but it is inconceivable that anyone arriving at the new airport would want to use it. *Hualampong* is on the other side of the city and the only train of the day to Pattaya departs at 6:50am. (There are no trains on weekends.) The fare is 31 *baht*. If you want a shower before boarding, there are good facilities in *Hualampong* for a cost of 10 *baht*. The rail journey to Pattaya takes about four hours and Pattaya Railway Station is a little out of town. There is usually a *Baht* Bus or two hanging around the station at the time of arrival and the fare to Central Pattaya will be upwards of 50 *baht* each. Train travel may be exciting for some people but, if you have just got off a long flight, the thought of crossing Bangkok to reach the station and taking possibly another six hours to get to Pattaya is ridiculous.

Places to Stay

Pattaya has many excellent hotels, apartments, and guesthouses. You can opt for one of the multi-star, big name hotels if that is your preference. Mid-range hotels are very good at 600 to 1,200 *baht* per night, depending on the season. Serviced, budget rooms starting at around 400 *baht* per night may be small but are usually clean and comfortable. If you plan to stay for a month or longer, apartments, guesthouses and pubs charging between 5,000 and 10,000 *baht* per month are very economical.

TIP
Be warned that some up-market hotels will charge you extra (between 500 and 800 baht) if you bring an 'overnight guest' back to your room. It is a good idea to ask at reception before booking in. According to the 'streetwise', a way to avoid this is to initially book into the hotel as a couple. If you are asked where your partner is, you can say you are meeting her later. (Not strictly a lie). NOTE: This ploy may or may not work as it has not been tested in the field by the author, although it worked well with laboratory mice. A problem may arise should an observant hotel employee notice that your companion on the second night is not the same as your lady of the first night.

I once asked at a very nice hotel if they charged extra for bringing a lady back for the night. The receptionist said no, that was not a problem. She then smiled and added, "But if you bring two lady back, we charge more." That's fair enough, don't you think?

TIP
If you are in Pattaya over the New Year period, some hotels 'require' that you pay (usually around 1,000 baht per person) to attend their New Year's Eve Party. This is whether you go or not. Again, check with reception first.

For experienced travellers, the following should be automatic but it needs to be reinforced anyway. Before booking any room, check it out. Feel the bed and switch on the fan and/or air conditioner, firstly to see if they actually work and secondly to see if they make any noise. There is nothing worse than trying to sleep with a noisy fan or air con clattering away all night. Check that the toilet flushes and the shower supplies adequate, clean water. Also check there is no karaoke bar or bar with a nightly live band nearby. Although the brick and cement plaster construction of most buildings is reasonably soundproof, the din from some drunk foreigner screaming 'My Way' at the top of his lungs can penetrate three feet of reinforced concrete. And Thai DJ's and bands know no volume setting apart from 'maximum'.

> ***TIP***
> *At any time of the year except perhaps around Christmas, ensure that you book a room with an air-conditioner. For anyone not used to the heat, fans just do not ease the discomfort or humidity. Rooms with air conditioners start at around 500 baht per night.*

Because hotels have been caught in the past by guests leaving without checking out, saying goodbye or paying the bill, most will insist on payment or partial payment in advance. If you are going to pay by credit card, they may wish to copy your card details. While they do this, do not let the card out of your sight.

> ***TIP***
> *If you are visiting Pattaya for the first time or are unfamiliar with the place, upon arrival at your hotel make sure you grab some of their business cards. Whenever you leave your room, take one of the cards with you. Why? Because you would not be the first farang who has forgotten the name of his hotel when he has ended up tired and emotional in the wee small hours of the morning.*
>
> *Strange place + grown man + alcohol = "What the hell is the name of my hotel?"*

Personal Safety

All countries have their share of dishonest people and some foreign tourist agencies warn that Pattaya has a reputation for being a less than safe destination for travellers. The Tourist Authority of Thailand claims Pattaya recveives more than 5 million visitors a year of which two-thirds are from abroad. Any place attracting that many tourists is likely to also attract nefarious types who follow the money. Criminal elements are certainly present as local newspaper reports will verify, but most of the violence is Thai v Thai so the average mug tourist, if he doesn't go looking for trouble, probably won't find any. Many foreigners will attest they have never felt unsafe or threatened while walking around Pattaya at any time of the day or night.

This is not to say that something untoward can not happen. Make personal safety Number One and use COMMON SENSE at all times. A bulging wallet in the back pocket is child's play for an expert pickpocket. Bag-snatchers and pickpockets prowl crowded places and a purse dangling from a wrist or shoulder is a tempting target for thieves who operate on foot or on motorcycles. If you do carry a bag, carry it on your side away from the road when walking alone or between the two of you when walking with a friend. This makes it more difficult for a speeding motorcyclist to snatch it from you.

> *His wife woke him at 3:30am to tell him that her monthly period had come on suddenly and she was out of panty-liners. Being a devoted husband, he got dressed and walked the short distance to Tops Supermarket to purchase some. Walking along Second Road on the way back to his room, a motorcycle carrying two youths sped past and the passenger snatched the plastic bag from his hand. A little shaken, he walked back to the supermarket and bought another pack.*
>
> *After telling his wife of the incident, she asked why he did not call the police.*
>
> *"What for?" he laughed. "It cost me 25 baht but I would pay 100 baht just to see the look on their faces once they stopped to see what goodies were in the bag."*

Don't walk alone in dimly lit areas at four o'clock in the morning. If your hotel has a room safe, then use it. If not, they may have a safety deposit facility where you can leave all your travel documents, valuables and extra money. Only carry enough money on you for your immediate needs and don't go flashing it about for the entire world to see. This is especially important if you have an 'overnight guest' in your room. Most hotel staff are honest, but the sight of a pile of cash sitting on the dressing table may be too much temptation for a desperate employee or Bar Hostess.

MONEY NUMBER ONE

TIP

If you hide money in a 'very safe place' in your room, don't forget where you put it! One guy accused his honest and bewildered female companion of stealing several thousand baht from his room. She denied it, he ranted and raved, the police were called and the situation became very nasty. Three days later, while dressing to go out, he noticed there was something stuffed into the toe of his shoe. He pulled out the wad of notes he had hidden while he was drunk and wrongly accused the girl of stealing.

Thailand has its share of confidence tricksters who come in a variety of shapes, sizes and nationalities. They are always very charming and usually approach you and engage in polite conversation. Many tourists see this as an excellent opportunity to talk and mix with a friendly local. The truth is that Thai people are naturally shy and rarely go out of their way to talk to foreigners. The golden rule is, if any person approaches you and appears overly eager and friendly with offers of help or advice, you can be fairly certain they are up to no good.

Be very wary of any person who desperately needs to 'borrow' money from you because of some misfortune that has recently befallen them. You will not get the money back no matter how sincere he or she appears to be or how pathetic the tale of woe.

Tony was drinking at a bar with his Thai wife. Shortly after she went off to get something to eat another Englishman, who called Tony by name, approached him and behaved as if they were lifelong friends. Tony could not recall ever meeting the guy but, when you meet people in bars, a lack of recollection can be easily explained. Anyway, he knew what hotel Tony was staying in and he bought a round of drinks. The guy went on to explain that he was in trouble as his girlfriend had left him and cleaned out his apartment and bank account. Could he borrow 1,000 baht until tomorrow? What is your room number? I'll bring it to your room before noon tomorrow. Thanks mate. He then paid his bill at the bar using the borrowed money and left. Later, Tony's lady returned and asked who was the farang he was speaking to. He said that he did not really know. Why do you ask? "Because," she answered, "he came up to me on the street and asked what your name was, what country you come from and what hotel we stay in."

Under Thai law, foreigners are required to carry their passport with them at all times. This is not unreasonable, since all Thai citizens over the age of 16 are required to carry identity cards. Should you get into trouble or be involved in an accident, it is the quickest way for authorities or hospital staff to identify you.

<u>TIP</u>
The problem is some foreigners find it inconvenient and often impractical to carry a valuable passport around 24 hours per day. If you have not already done so, take a colour photocopy of the personal information page (the one with your photo). Some people have the copy laminated to protect it from wear and tear. On arrival in Thailand, take a photocopy (black and white will do) of the Departure (T.M.) Card, the page with your current visa (if any) and the page containing your entry stamp. With your passport locked safely away, should you be asked to show it, the combination of the above will usually suffice, although it is strictly illegal. It would be rare but you could still be fined.

The main danger in Pattaya is from cars and motorcycles. Be careful when walking around as many of the streets are devoid of footpaths. If they do exist, the footpaths are often taken up with stalls, hawkers, goods of all description or parked motorcycles and cars. This forces the pedestrian to use the roadway. Do not think, just because the road is ONE WAY, that motorcycle riders can not come at you from the other direction. Motorcycles go everywhere in Pattaya - on footpaths, beaches, up stairs, down escalators, through restaurants. Nothing is impossible for a motorcycle. Crossing a road is particularly dangerous. Look in every direction, not just towards the oncoming traffic, never be in a hurry and ALWAYS give Thai drivers RIGHT OF WAY. Only one car in a thousand will stop and allow you to cross the street safely.

If you think that the danger from motorcycles is a joke, take a note of all the ladies with scars on their arms and/or legs and politely ask them how they got the scar. In ninety-eight percent of cases, the scar will be the result of a motorcycle accident.

MONEY NUMBER ONE

At 3:00am, the four girls fought over which one of them would drive the motorcycle they were all attempting to ride. They were all blind drunk and the argument was over which of them was the least drunk. Eventually a decision was made and, with not a safety helmet in sight, the giggling quartet mounted the 125cc bike for the trip home.

In 2002, the *Bangkok Post* reported:
"A new study suggests many Thai motorcycle owners are simply accidents waiting to happen. The survey is by *Chulalongkor*n University, Honda Motors and the US Head Protection Research Laboratory. Here is what it says: 90% of motorcyclists in accidents have had no bike-riding training, just one in a thousand have passed any sort of recognised driving course and four of ten are drunk."

The farang went to renew his comprehensive motorcycle insurance and was surprised to find the annual premium less than the year before. He was told it was his no claim bonus. He asked if many customers received the no claim bonus to which the clerk responded, "No. You first one!"

Travelling About

Unless you are the driver, never sit where you have an uninterrupted view of the road ahead. As one wit put it;
"I want to die peacefully in my sleep like my grandmother
- not screaming in terror like the passengers in her car!"

As soon as possible after arriving, obtain a map and familiarize yourself with the layout of the city. It is unbelievably easy to find your way around. In simplistic terms, if you find yourself on a major ONE WAY road and you can see the ocean, you are on Pattaya Beach Road; if you cannot see the ocean you are on Pattaya Second Road. Many free magazines and other publications available in hotels or tourist agencies contain maps and provide plenty of tourist information if you are looking for new and interesting places to go.

Pattaya's transport and traffic problems are growing in proportion to its population and are a source of continuous headaches for those responsible for solving them. For instance, in 2004 a six-month trial of a free bus service began whereby six air-conditioned buses were to travel set routes including the Beach Road-Second Road one-way circuit. A special bus lane was marked and a number of bus stops were designated along the route. After only three days of operation, an urgent meeting was called between city officials and the Pattaya *Baht* Bus Collective. A representative pointed out that since the start of the service, passenger numbers were down dramatically and drivers were facing financial hardship. City officials bowed to pressure from the *Baht* Bus Collective and reduced the trial period to three months, after which a 30 *baht* fixed charge for the service was imposed.

Alas, this bus service no longer exists. The 30 *baht* was too expensive for locals and the service too infrequent to be convenient for tourists. The mobile tourist is left with five options:

Metered Taxis

Pattaya finally has a metered taxi service which began in 2008. The comfortable blue and gold vehicles usually congergate outside the main shopping centres such as Big C, Royal Garden, Central Festival shopping mall and Villa Market. The sign on the roof says 'Taxi-Meter' but don't push it. From all reports the drivers don't like using the meter (if they actually have one) and would rather quote you a fare to your destination. Naturally, this fare is far over and above what it would cost using the meter. Some drivers will simply refuse to take you if you insist on using the meter so be warned. Still, the vehicles are comfortable and a step in the right direction.

Baht Buses

In spite of the militancy of some of the drivers, *Baht* Buses, also called '*Baht* Taxis' (in Thai '*rot song taew*' which literally means 'car with two rows [of seats]'), are an efficient and cheap means of getting around. Nevertheless, *Baht* Buses figure prominently in conversations amongst foreigners, both tourists and expats alike. For many years, foreign language newspapers printed letters from disgruntled foreigners complaining about being ripped-off by the drivers. Many complaints to the Tourist Police were about the same matter.

Inside each vehicle a sign outlined the maximum fares payable. The sign stated: 'The regular fare of mini bus in Pattaya is not over 10 *baht* per person according to the law of enforced by the department of land transport' (*sic*). The problem was that, due to the generosity, benevolence and gooey-gooey niceness of Pattaya's *Baht* Taxi drivers, they only charged their Thai

MONEY NUMBER ONE

passengers 5 *baht*. The hard-working, taxpaying, law-abiding Thai citizens were given a 50% discount while foreigners paid the correct maximum fare. (Naturally, a Thai travelling with a *farang* companion was also required to pay the higher fare so the driver could be seen to be evenhanded and not because he knew the *farang* would be paying for his companion's trip anyway.) Many visitors accepted this as being the 'Thai price' as opposed to the '*farang* price' but just as many saw it as a blatant rip-off.

But you can scream 'racism' or 'discrimination' until you are blue in the face and it will do you no good. You can quote the UN Charter, the Thai Constitution or the Geneva Convention and it will do you no good. The sign says the fare is 'not over 10 *baht*' and the driver is free to give a discount to whomever he chooses.

With the dramatic rise in world oil prices between 2006 and 2008, the cost of fuel in Thailand almost trippled and most drivers began charging their Thai passengers 10 *baht* as well. Towards the end of 2008 oil prices plummeted but the drivers did not reduce their fares. Now everybody, Thai and foreigners alike, pays 10 *baht* per person and the problem has dissolved. (It is truly ironic that the demise of fare discrimination in Pattaya came about not because of an attack of guilt, a sense of fairness nor even common sense, but as a result of OPEC!)

TIP

1. *Avoid getting on a Baht Bus that does not already have passengers on it. The reasoning behind it is that the driver may demand a higher fare by saying he made a special trip for you and taken you somewhere he had not intended to go.*
2. *Make sure you always carry small change with you, particularly 10 baht coins. You would be surprised just how many drivers do not have change for your 50 or 100 baht notes.*
3. *When you reach your destination, press the buzzer as late as possible so that the taxi stops a short distance past where you actually wanted to get off. Pay for your ride by placing the exact fare into the driver's hand. Don't look at him, don't ask how much he wants, don't ask if the fare is correct, don't talk, don't discuss, don't argue, don't barter. Simply hand over the money, turn around, check for traffic and walk back to your destination. At this point, should he want to discuss the matter with you, he will have to either*

MONEY NUMBER ONE

> *leave the vehicle or reverse against the flow of traffic. The drivers very rarely do this, especially if there are other passengers in the vehicle. NEVER get into an argument or altercation with the driver.*
>
> 4 *Avoid boarding the taxis waiting outside supermarkets, shopping centres and bus stations, particularly those parked outside Royal Garden, Big C, Central Festival and the Jomtien-bound ones on Second Road outside the school at South Pattaya. If you and your party are the only passengers, they may charge extra as if for a private hire. At other times they usually wait until they have a full load of passengers. This can take a while. (Define 'full'? When the weight of passengers causes the rear axle to scrape the roadway.) You are better off walking past these stationary vehicles and flagging down a taxi already in motion.*

For travel on a *Baht* Bus plying a set route within the confines of Pattaya City, it is not necessary to negotiate the fare beforehand. The moment you speak to a driver about the fare or ask a question regarding your destination, the price goes up. In this respect, it is a good idea to quickly familiarize yourself with the routes the buses take. The system is not complicated.

> *A farang with his beautiful Thai girlfriend approached the driver of a Baht Bus travelling along Second Road and negotiated a fare to the Dusit Hotel. The farang bargained the driver down to 40 baht each and looked pleased with himself as he and his girlfriend took their seats. His understandably shy companion did not intercede to help her farang boyfriend out, even though she would probably have known where the Dusit Hotel was and what the fare should have been. (This is not uncommon. She may have been overjoyed at the prospect of helping out a financially-strapped fellow countryman. You will learn more about this behaviour in a later chapter.) Had the farang taken the time to look at a map, he would have known that the taxi was going to go right past the Dusit in any case and the correct fare was no more than 10 baht per person.*

For travel on a *Baht* Bus from Pattaya to Naklua or Jomtien, the fare is 10 *baht* (20 *baht* as far as the terminus) for both Thais and foreigners. To hire a *Baht* Bus to take you, and your party, exclusively to a particular destination or somewhere outside the Naklua-Pattaya-Jomtien area, it *is* necessary to negotiate the fare beforehand. Do a bit of haggling up front and don't automatically accept their first offer.

Motorcycle Taxi

These are easily recognizable as the drivers wear a coloured vest with a number and sometimes the name of his/her home base written on the back. They cost more than the *Baht* Buses as they offer an express door-to-door service but I have had no experience of drivers wanting to charge me a '*farang* price'. The minimum charge has risen from 20 to 30 *baht*, but always settle on the price before you start. Because this is the least safe means of transport, if you are not motorcycle-friendly, use it only as a last resort. Many accidents and near-accidents involve motorcycles and, by law, you must be provided with a safety helmet. Make sure you wear it.

Vehicles for Hire

There is an abundance of cars, pick-ups and motorcycles of all description and sizes for rent in Pattaya. If you disregard STRONG advice not to drive any vehicle in Thailand then shop around for the best deal, but make sure you have either a Thai Driver's License or a valid International Driver's License obtained *outside* of Thailand and take out solid, watertight insurance. You may be asked to leave your passport with the rental agency as a security measure. Never do this! Make a photocopy if necessary, but never hand over your passport to anyone except a uniformed police officer or other legitimate Thai authorities. If the owner refuses to rent you a vehicle without your passport as security, find one who will. In the company of the owner/hirer, check the vehicle for any marks, dents or scratches before parting with your money. Check the fuel gauge as well. In most cases, the vehicle will have to be returned with a full fuel tank.

On average, 2.3 people are killed per day in traffic accidents in and around Pattaya so, before you decide whether to drive or not, sit for five minutes and watch the traffic mayhem in the streets. It can be a very sobering experience and you may be excused for thinking that many road users appear to have no fear of death.

MONEY NUMBER ONE

Even if you consider yourself to be a good driver, statistics correctly point out that foreigners are involved in a disproportionately high number of reported traffic accidents. Foreign drivers are often ignorant of Thai road rules, or mistakenly believe there are none, and pose a danger to both themselves and the law-abiding road users.

Always drive under the assumption that, should your vehicle be involved in a traffic accident, any accident, it is likely to be your fault. Why? Because if you hadn't been there, the accident wouldn't have happened. *Duhhh!* The police can withhold your passport until you settle with the owners of other vehicles involved. If your visa subsequently expires, you have an added 'overstay' problem and can be jailed. Injured parties will expect to be paid the costs of medical treatment plus substantial compensation. The cost of repairs, medical treatment and/or legal representation *will* be astronomical.

Walking

Pattaya is possibly not as pedestrian-friendly as it should be. Although walking is good exercise and you get to see more of the finer points of the place, Pattaya has a temporary shortage of pedestrian-exclusive footpaths. In spite of continuous and applauded efforts by authorities to beautify and upgrade the bountiful charms of this quality city, where walkways do exist they are often narrow, uneven, potted or loaded with obstacles for the unwary. Be patient and careful.

Desperate thieves have stolen some of the thousands of metal drain covers throughout the city, leaving deep, dangerous and often unmarked holes for the unwary. Although they are continually being replaced, avoid walking on any of the existing covers because the metal in some of the older ones may be corroded or the concrete may have deteriorated, leaving them unsafe when weight is applied. Your 45kg Thai girlfriend may experience no problem but the cover may give way under a 100kg plus *farang* frame. Jagged steel and concrete makes a mess of human flesh. There is no 'public liability' here so, should you injure yourself falling into an open excavation, pothole or a drain, your medical bills are your problem. For litigation-happy American readers, if you think you will be able to sue anybody for damages, think again.

Whenever forced to walk along the edge of a road, make it a point to always walk against the flow of traffic. Not totally foolproof but it does allow you to anticipate potential problems and affords time to take evasive action if necessary. More importantly, it provides the opportunity to look directly into the homicidal eyes of the mad motorcyclist just before he sends you to oblivion.

One final warning. In most Western countries, a pedestrian crossing means the pedestrian has right-of-way and vehicles must stop. However, in some parts of the world, pedestrian crossings are only there because once the workers marking the centre line and other lanes had finished, a lot of white paint was left over. Rather than waste it, they got the idea of painting zebra crossings on the road just like the pictures in foreign magazines. You could find yourself severely dead if you believe that any vehicle will automatically stop for you at a pedestrian/zebra crossing in Pattaya.

Money

Yes, you will need to bring some of this with you if your holiday in Thailand is to be a success. How much you bring depends on you. How you bring it also depends on you, but here is a quick summary of the alternatives.

Cash

This is the simplest way to bring your money as all major foreign currencies can be exchanged at the banks or currency exchanges. However, it is the least safe way.

1   DON'T bring wads of cash with you unless you have confidence in your ability to protect it.
2   LEAVE all but the money required for your immediate needs in your room safe or hotel's safety deposit box.
3   DON'T ever leave money 'hidden' in your hotel room.
4   DON'T ever go walking around with half the Bank of England in your wallet.
5   DON'T advertise your wealth or go flashing it about.
6   FIND a secure place on your person to keep your wallet and/or cash. Remember that a thick wallet hanging out of your back pocket is a tempting and very easy target for a skilled thief.

MONEY NUMBER ONE

TIP
If you are going to bring US currency, make sure the notes are not torn and that you do not have any US100 dollar bills in the 1990-93 series. Apparently, there are so many forgeries of these particular notes that banks and money changers in Pattaya no longer accept them.

TIP
Airports and hotels sometimes offer the worst exchange rates. The hotels of Pattaya are no exception. Better rates are available from banks and Currency Exchanges along the street.

Traveller's Cheques

These are much safer than cash because they can be cancelled and replaced if lost or stolen. Some people find them to be a little inconvenient because:

1. Not all places accept traveller's cheques.
2. When purchasing them, there is often a fee.
3. When exchanging them, there may be a commission.
4. To spend or exchange them, you need to show your passport. As mentioned earlier, it is not a good idea for foreigners to carry their passport around.

ATM and Credit Cards

An internationally linked credit or debit ATM card is much more convenient. Pattaya has an abundance of 24-hour ATM outlets that accept a variety of cards and have simple English language operating instructions. Most will dispense a maximum of 20 notes per transaction which equates to 20,000 *baht*. If the machine runs out of 1,000 *baht* notes, it will dispense twenty 500 *baht* notes totalling 10,000 *baht*. Some precautions and pitfalls you should be aware of:

1. BEFORE leaving home, check with your bank that your card will be accepted in Thailand.
2. COPY down all the details of your account (NOT your PIN number), the details on your card and the emergency telephone number in the case of a lost or stolen card. Keep this in a safe place. Photocopying the front of your card is a good idea.

3. DON'T rely on one credit card or account as your sole source of funds while you are here. Have a backup plan, spare cash or another ATM or credit card in case your primary card is lost or stolen. It has been known for some of the older ATM machines to damage the magnetic strip on some plastic cards. If this happens, the card is useless. Being broke and a long way from home is no fun.
4. THINK ahead. Don't ever assume that you will just be able to stroll down to the nearest ATM and get money any time you need it. Electronic systems are notoriously tempermental and machines here sometimes have 'communication' problems or run out of money. This is most prevalent on Sunday nights or the first and last days of each month (Thai pay days).
5. DON'T go to the ATM and withdraw bundles of cash at three or four o'clock in the morning, especially if you are drunk or alone. That is asking for trouble.
6. DO NOT let your credit card out of your sight when paying either in the hotel or when shopping. Credit card fraud is rife in many countries, with fake cards being produced in vast numbers. The personal details of the real card can be downloaded onto a computer and 'clone' cards produced. Other common methods include making more than one receipt or asking the customer to sign twice as the first attempt "didn't come through". Credit card companies say the most vulnerable time for customers is when their card is taken away by a sales assistant for 'checking' and senior Pattaya police urge credit card holders to insist on not being parted from their property during the transaction process.
7. DO NOT let any friendly passerby help you if you are having trouble with an ATM withdrawal. A gang of foreigner criminals operated by waiting near an ATM and offering 'assistance' to tourists. One had a card reader concealed in his palm which electronically copied all the details of your account (including the PIN) which would be used almost immediately to produce a 'clone' card. By the time you realized it, your account had been emptied.

MONEY NUMBER ONE

Food

The food in Thailand is as delicious as it is varied. It is rightfully the world's number one cuisine. The fresh fruit available from street vendors is particularly delicious. But no matter what your taste, every country boasting food worth eating is represented by at least one restaurant in Pattaya. If you like it hot, then the Thai food is excellent and relatively inexpensive. Anyone not used to eating spicy (hot) food should take it slowly to begin with as it could take a few days to acclimatize. Chillies are not only hot going down, but also hot coming out, if you get my meaning.

TIP
For the adventurous tourist, there is an interesting array of deep-fried insects that many Thais are quite fond of. The fried grasshoppers require plenty of liquid (beer is the best) to wash them down. The black water beetles and other creepy-crawlies are an acquired taste. Advice from experienced travellers is to be careful eating uncooked vegetables, salads etc., and of course, do not drink the tap water. Bottled water is both cheap and plentiful.

There are excellent supermarkets in Pattaya: 'Big C' shopping centres on Second Road opposite *Soi 2*, on *Sukhumvit* Road near the intersection with South Pattaya Road and one, 'Big C Extra', on Central Road near the intersection with Third Road. 'Foodland' is on Central Road. 'Tops Supermarket' and 'Best Supermarket' are in Central Pattaya at the intersection of Second Road and Central Road. Tesco/Lotus shopping complexes are on Pattaya North Road and near the intersection of *Thepprasit* Road and *Sukhumvit* Road. 'Friendship Supermarket' is on South Pattaya Road not far from the intersection with *Soi Buakow*, while 'Villa Market' is on Second Road opposite *Soi 13*. A new addition is Central Festival shopping mall between *Sois* 9 and 10 and Beach and Second Roads. As well as these major outlets, there are innumerable 7-Eleven's, Family Mart's and general stores conveniently situated all around town which can be used for emergencies and the essentials – booze, cigarettes and condoms.

Drugs

If you value your life, health and freedom, have nothing to do with illegal drugs. Some ill-informed foreigners have suggested that many Pattaya Bar Hostesses take methamphetamines to keep them thin and active and, in 2002, a newspaper reported that an estimated 100,000 methamphetamine pills were consumed daily in Chonburi province.

As in most other countries in this world, drugs can probably be found if you go out and look. My strong advice is not to look. If you are into that type of activity, stay out of Thailand, because severe penalties are in place if you are caught. With all the other enjoyable activities abounding in Pattaya, the only drug you should possibly consider is Viagra.

> *Viagra, is available over the counter at many pharmacies and some hotels for 500 baht per 100mg tablet. Reliable information suggests that 'copy Viagra' can also be purchased on the street for between 300 and 600 baht per pack of four. Make sure you consult a doctor first, especially if you have heart problems or are hypoglycemic.*

Don't be fooled into participating in any illicit narcotic activity. At the least, you could be conned out of a few hundred *baht*. At its most serious, you could easily be set up for a 'sting' operation which works along the following lines: Once you make a drug purchase, you are apprehended by an accomplice of the seller posing as a police officer and threatened with all sorts of horrors. The seller then approaches you saying that he can 'fix' things with the police for anywhere between 20,000 and 100,000 *baht*. You have the choice of either paying this ransom or spending a very uncomfortable time in Thailand for much longer than you had planned. I have also been told that many drug sellers are in fact police informants. Once the drugs are in your possession, you will be apprehended by real police officers.

As an added disincentive to consume drugs, police conduct random urine testing operations targeting bars and, in particular, nightclubs and discos. Tourists and Thais alike are required to provide a urine sample and kiss goodbye to your holiday if your test is positive.

MONEY NUMBER ONE

STD's and AIDS

The World Health Organisation keeps statistics regarding the number of people in Thailand supposedly infected with STD's and those who have been diagnosed with HIV. The Thai government and private organisations have made virtuous and successful efforts to slow the spread of sexually transmitted diseases through education and the promotion of safe sex practices. Do not believe the rubbish spread by Pattaya-haters that Aids is rampant in the city.

The Bar Hostesses do not want STD or HIV infections any more than you do, but you may occasionally find a sex worker who has limited knowledge of disease prevention.

> *One G.R.O. ('Guest Relations Officer' equivalent to 'Bar Hostess') in the Philippines was heard to say that in order to prevent STD's, HIV and pregnancy, she gave herself a thorough washing immediately after any sexual activity. Her mother passed that little gem of information on to her and her fourteen brothers and sisters.*

Health certificates testifying that the holder is STD-free are not worth the paper they are written on because fraudulent ones can be purchased very cheaply. Even if genuine, the certificate is only really good at the time the blood test was taken. One hour later, he or she could have had unprotected sex and contracted something.

> ### *TIP*
> *As a general rule, wherever you may be in the world, never have sex with someone who does not **insist** that you use a condom. If she does not insist with you, then it's a safe bet that she also did not insist with those who came before you. (Excuse the pun.)*

Although condom use still may not be 100% safe, it is certainly safer than not using one. Condoms can be purchased at almost every supermarket and 24-hour convenience store in Pattaya so there is no excuse. ALWAYS PLAY SAFE.

Health & Medical

Although, at the time of writing, no immunisations are officially required for travel to Thailand, it may be advisable to consult your doctor a few months before departing your home. He or she may recommend certain precautionary injections.

If you are unfortunate enough to require medical attention while here, there are excellent hospitals, doctors, dentists, opticians and pharmacies in Pattaya. Many medical practitioners were trained overseas and speak English. Let's hope you never need to find out, but the medical treatment you would receive here is good.

Having said that, whether you are paying a short visit or planning on a long stay, it is STRONGLY advised you take out medical insurance before arriving. For holidays less than a month in duration, it may be possible to get some form of medical coverage through your Travel Agent. If you already have medical insurance in your home country, make certain that it also covers you whilst overseas.

1. MAKE SURE you have hospital coverage. Although the hospitals in Thailand are excellent, in-patient services or prolonged hospitalisation can be very expensive. Out-patient treatment for minor ailments is probably not worth insuring as it likely won't break your budget.
2. CHECK with your insurer before departure which hospitals in Thailand will accept their coverage. Ask for a list of of those hospitals with an accepted record of dealing with your insurer. Some hospitals won't accept certain insurance companies and some insurance companies won't deal with certain hospitals.
3. FIND OUT if you would be required to pay the hospital account yourself and then claim it back from your insurance company once you return home. If so, ask what DOCUMENTATION you are required to have in order for your insurance company to reimburse you.
4. BRING your insurance card and explanatory documentation with you. Some hospitals will ask to see proof of your insurance coverage before you are admitted or else demand your credit card and/or a large cash deposit in lieu.
5. CARRY your insurance card (or photocopy thereof) with you at all times. Keep this with the photocopy of the identity page of your passport you should already have.

MONEY NUMBER ONE

It is also advised that if you ever fall ill with a stomach complaint (vomiting, diarrhoea, severe stomach pains etc), consult a doctor immediately. It may turn out to be a simple case of food poisoning, but the symptoms could also be an indication of something more serious. In the case of severe diarrhoea, insist the doctor test you for cholera which is fast-acting and can be contracted from something as simple as ingesting contaminated water on a fresh lettuce leaf. Cholera can be deadly if not treated quickly. If you are bitten by an animal - any animal - see a doctor immediately. Rabies still exists in South East Asia and it is better to be safe than sorry.

Should you need dental work or require new prescription glasses, check the prices around town. Visitors often find the rates here are much cheaper than for the same service in their own countries.

> *One guy needing extensive dental work was quoted thousands of pounds for the treatment in the UK. In Pattaya, he was quoted thousands of baht for the same procedure. He ended up getting all his dental work done here in Pattaya plus had a three-week holiday for less than it would have cost him for just the dental treatment alone in the UK.*

Laser eye surgery is big business in Thailand and much cheaper than in the West. Those people I have spoken to who have had laser treatments here have all been happy with the results.

Many pharmaceuticals which require a prescription in your home country can be purchased legally over the counter in pharmacies here. If you do take ongoing medication, it may be worth checking out the prices here for the same medication. Might be an idea to bring your doctor's prescription with you and have it ready just in case you are questioned by customs inspectors at the airport when you arrive home. Remember, many customs forms require you to declare any pharmaceuticals you may be bringing into the country.

Returning to the Airport

The return trip from Pattaya to either *Suvarnabhumi* or *Don Muang* Airport is easy. Minibuses, charging from 400 *baht,* can be booked from any hotel or travel agency and will pick you up from wherever you are staying and take you direct to the airport. The first one departs at 6:00am and the last one at 7:00pm but make sure you book at least a day in advance. Be warned, these minibuses are almost always full (eleven passengers) so if you don't appreciate being packed like a sardine, this may not be the option for you.

The heavily-advertised 24-hour taxi services to the airports should cost 800 *baht* plus the motorway tolls. Some operators have been known to overcharge so, before booking or handing over any money, confirm what the TOTAL fare will be. Again, operators like the taxi to be full so you may find yourself sharing with one or two other people.

Private taxis can be found and the fare to *Suvarnabhumi* will be between 1,000 and 1,500 *baht*. These you don't have to share with anybody.

Buses leave for *Suvarnabhumi* Airport from Jomtien Bus Station at 9:00am, 1:00pm, 5:00pm and 7:30pm.

From Pattaya North Road Bus Station, Bell Travel Service provides buses to *Suvarnabhumi* Airport at 6:00am, 9:00am, 11:00am, 1:00pm, 3:00pm, 5:00pm and 7:00pm, for a fare of 250 *baht*.

Most airlines require passengers to check in two hours before their flight so, whichever method you choose, leave Pattaya a good five hours before your flight departure time.

From mid-2007, paying the 500 *baht* Departure Tax before going through airport Immigration is no longer required. Don't worry, the tax still exists (risen to 750 *baht*), but is now included in the price of your ticket.

4
People of Many Faces

Thais are a gentle, wonderful and multifaceted people. Even though they have a rich culture dating back thousands of years, it is often difficult for foreigners to rationalize their sometimes idiosyncratic behaviour. What may seem strange, oddball, confusing or illogical to ignorant foreigners has a simple explanation - "This is Thailand!" But Pattaya is not typical of Thailand. Books on Thai culture may be accurate when referring to the general population, but the people who work in this major tourist destination can prove the exception to many rules.

> *The foreigner decided to move to Pattaya but, being cautious, asked his expat friend, "Living in Pattaya, what are the pros and cons?"*
> *His friend casually replied, "A somewhat broad but accurate description of the population."*

Consequently, before you interact with the local inhabitants, there are some lessons to be learned. The following insights are gleaned from the cumulative experience of Pattaya's expat community and, as we all know, experience is something you don't get until just after you need it.

Lesson One – Pattaya is Different

Thailand is an extremely diverse country comprised of four distinct regions; the North, the Northeast, Bangkok and the South. Anyone who has spent any length of time in Bangkok could be forgiven for thinking Bangkok Thais are a different race of people altogether. They are more affluent, more educated, more confident and much more cosmopolitan than Thais throughout the rest of the country. They speak close to textbook Thai and, with experience and a good ear, it is possible to detect a Bangkok accent when you hear one. A good example of the Thai language spoken correctly, i.e. Bangkok Thai, is provided by Thai newsreaders on the television.

Bangkok has been at the international crossroads of Asia for so long that the inhabitants have an almost blasé attitude towards foreigners. In most cases, foreigners are treated no differently to other Thais. You could live there a year and never hear the word *farang* used to describe either youself or other foreigners.

Bangkok is home to the majority of Thailand's middle classes but, rightly or wrongly, Bangkok Thais consider themselves the social elite of Thailand. Rural Thais consider them to be snobs and the resulting class distinction has been the cause of many political problems in the country.

The rural Thais of the populous northeast area known as Isaan mostly speak a "low class" version of Thai with a sprinkle of Lao or Cambodian words and phrases. It is said they "speak Isaan". These people are neither worldly nor affluent and their attitude towards foreigners is poles apart from that of the residents of Bangkok.

Then there is Pattaya, a city 'owned' by the elite of Bangkok, populated by the rural poor of Isaan and loosely controlled by a mixed bag of Thai mafioso fuelled on corruption. As if placing a hundred thousand farmers into an alien urban environment is not confusing enough, add a few million foreign visitors each year. Pattaya is a place where the country meets the city and East meets West, making it a recipe for chaos.

Generally speaking, Pattaya locals don't understand their Thai 'masters', they understand foreigners even less, but they are envious and contemptuous of both.

MONEY NUMBER ONE

Lesson Two – Nationalism

Thailand is the only country in Southeast Asia that has never been colonized. Through political mastery and clever diplomacy at the height of colonial interference in Asia, the Thai successfully kept the two most powerful Imperialist powers in the region - the English in India, Burma and Malaya and the French in Indochina (Vietnam and Cambodia) - apart and thus maintained Thai independence and spared the country from foreign domination. For the English and the French, Thailand became a buffer zone between their respective Asian colonial empires. At the outbreak of World War II, Thailand was the only Asian nation to voluntarily ally with Japan, a political tactic which saved the country from possible destruction.

Since World War II, generally speaking, the Thais have managed to keep the rest of the world at arm's length. Sure, the history books tell us the country has had years of internal political upheaval and turmoil (there have been eighteen coups in just over sixty years) and suffered economic problems, but the Thai people have slowly modernized their country - their way. Thais don't welcome foreigners sticking their noses into what they perceive as strictly Thai affairs.

"What does this have to do with me having a great time in Thailand?" you may ask. Well, you will have a much easier time here if you always remember, when dealing with the Thai people, they are extremely proud and nationalistic. They love Thailand and despite their outward friendliness and 'Thai smile', generally do not care much for foreigners. They only like things that are Thai - Thai food, Thai music, Thai culture, Thai traditions and Thai thinking. The people believe in their cultural superiority.

Don't meddle in Thai business. If your girlfriend is involved in a heated argument or even a fight with another Thai, stay the hell out of it. Never forget, that delicate little flower beside you, the one who has managed to capture your heart, no matter what she does or where she lives, no matter how she dresses or how she speaks, is now and will always be, 100% THAI.

Finally, keep your opinions to yourself because a quick way to get a Thai off side is to criticize his country or his way of life. A "back home we do this" or "back home it's like that" type of guy makes no friends here. If you do not absorb anything else in this book, know this to be true: NEVER, at any time, anywhere, under any circumstances, even if only in jest, say, write or repeat anything which could be misunderstood, misquoted, misinterpreted or taken out of context to be considered even slightly derogatory to any Thai person or the country itself. DON'T SAY YOU HAVE NOT BEEN WARNED.

Lesson Three - Smiling

A very successful advertising campaign declared Thailand to be 'The Land of Smiles'. Much has already been written about the 'Thai smile' which has become less visible over the past decade. Sadly, for reasons unknown, Thais are not smiling like they used to. The important thing to realize is that a Thai, smiling, may not necessarily indicate the same thing it does when you or I smile. Westerners smile to convey happiness, amusement or a pleasant greeting. A Thai smile can mean these things as well, but it can also mean 'please', 'thank you', 'goodbye', 'excuse me', 'I'm sorry', 'I don't know' or simply 'yes'. It can also be a way of hiding embarrassment, avoiding confrontation or easing the tension if a situation looks to be getting too heated.

> *The foreigner and his Thai girlfriend had a heated argument one day. The argument was basically one-sided as he ranted and raved. With his blood pressure just about to blast him into lunar orbit, he looked at her – and she was smiling. This enraged him even more and he shouted at her, "Do you think this is funny?"*
> *To cut a long story short, he calmed down, she made an insincere apology and they made up. He came to realize that she had been smiling, not because his tirade was amusing her, but because she was trying to ease the tension. Jai yen yen!*
> *At least, he **hoped** that's why she was smiling.*

This tactic works both ways so, if you are ever stopped by a Thai policeman for some perceived infraction, do not get angry. Giving him a big, broad, continuous smile will work wonders.

Lesson Four - Lying

You must always remember that Pattaya is Fantasyland and should not be taken too seriously. As well as telling lies for the all the usual reasons, Asian people will sometimes lie to avoid an unpleasant situation or to avoid 'losing face'. The book *Thailand Fever* sums it up the following way:

> *"Telling the truth is desirable in Thailand, but it is just not as important as protecting the face of those for whom Thais feel respect ... Many Thais clearly believe there is such a thing as a 'noble lie', and they*

MONEY NUMBER ONE

are able to tell one with a minimum of guilt if it seems it will help them or someone they respect avoid a confrontation or hurt feelings. What's more, other Thais will generally respect their decision to lie if it helps save face for someone else."

They also want to keep you happy and if this involves telling a lie, then so be it. When you later discover that they have been less than forthright, they are usually not around to argue with.

A few years ago, an enterprising but misguided fellow brought a lie detector with him to Pattaya. Unfortunately it blew every fuse and blacked out half of the city less than five minutes into his first interrogation. He may have been better off bringing a truth detector which would have required a lot less electricity since it would only light up when someone actually told the truth.

Sometimes, people will not actually lie in the strict Biblical sense of the word. They will simply not tell the full truth. If someone answers your question with a noncommittal response of "maybe", "sometimes" or "perhaps", it usually means that the actual answer is one that you do not want to hear. In a conversation she may tell you only the things that you want to hear and conveniently leave out anything she thinks you will not like, no matter how important the information could be to you. This strategy seems to work quite well. When they do happen to tell an outright blatant lie, there is no limit to their imagination.

Once upon a time, there was a guy who worked as a cook. One day his employer decided to entertain guests and ordered a roast chicken to be prepared for the meal. The cook himself was very hungry but was forbidden to eat. Eventually the smell of the roasting chicken got the better of him and, unable to contain his hunger any longer, he ate one of the legs. When he served up the chicken, minus one leg, his boss was furious and demanded to know what happened to the missing appendage. The cook replied that the chicken only had one leg to begin with. This obvious bullshit made his boss even angrier and he started beating the cook to force a confession. Even after a savage battering (excuse the pun), the cook still stuck to his 'one-legged chicken' story.

In Pattaya, even though you will hear many 'one-legged chicken' stories, it is to be hoped that you, dear reader, would never think of tinkering with the affections of your wonderful Thai companion by considering being other than 100% honest with her. Regrettably, many *farang* do not possess those high moral standards.

Lesson Five – Reasoning and Logic

An old gag goes like this: *There are two theories for arguing with a woman. Neither of them work.* All jokes aside, it is often difficult for Europeans to understand the wisdom and reasoning Asian people use to address a problem. Their logic differs from the way Westerners are taught to think.

> *He told his girlfriend he would call her but something came up and he was unable to call as arranged. When he phoned her the next evening, she was angry, saying that she waited up until 2:00am for his call. He apologized and explained that it was unavoidable. She told him that during the day she went out to play cards and proceeded to lose 5,000 baht. She only played because she was angry with him. It was therefore his fault that she lost the money.*

Thai people are pragmatic, intelligent and ingenious. Just because she may not have a university education, don't ever think that your beautiful Thai companion is not smart.

> *It would be her first time on an aeroplane and, before boarding their flight from Bangkok to Phnom Penh, his girlfriend asked him how far it was. He replied it was about the same distance as from Bangkok to Nong Khai. She then asked how long it would take. He answered that the flight should take just over an hour. She thought for a moment before casually remarking, "Mmm ... must be no traffic."*

I respect Bar Hostesses far more than I respect any politicians, but in some ways Bar Hostesses are like politicians. As such, never underestimate her ability to worm her way into or weasel her way out of sticky situations with a logic that defies imagination.

MONEY NUMBER ONE

A foreigner arrived back at his apartment to find the bedroom door blocked from the inside by a wardrobe. He forced his way in to discover his girlfriend in a semi-clothed state with a Thai man who was equally poorly attired. Angrily, he threw the guy out, using as much physical persuasion as he could muster. When he then confronted her, his girlfriend tearfully explained that the man was actually her brother who had paid her a surprise visit. On noticing a foul odour coming from somewhere in the bedroom, they both investigated and began moving furniture around in order to find the source. It was then that the apartment's power failed and, with no air conditioning, the pair decided to remove excess clothing in order to keep cool as they worked.

Ah, Mr Ripley, where are you when we need you? As any Pattaya expat will tell you, the number of concerned brothers visiting their sisters in this town is only exceeded by the number of monoped fowls hopping along Beach Road.

TIP
Never give a Bar Hostess time to think about any proposition you may make to her. Given twenty-four hours to mull it over, she will consult with her sorority of friends – the brain trust – who will put their collective heads together and like Baldrick (in the British comedy series Black Adder), come up with 'a cunning plan'. Guaranteed, the result will cost you money. As a general rule, the less time she has to think over your proposition, the more chance her response will be in your favour.

Lesson Six - Promises

Many men will tell you that women have excellent selective memories. The term 'selective' is used because anything they perceive to be to their benefit they remember, anything else, they conveniently forget. The wonderful Bar Hostesses of Pattaya have universally perfect memories. Be very careful what you say or what you promise, because they will not forget it. You could find yourself having to make good something that you had merely mentioned in jest or said when you were blind drunk.

His girlfriend wanted him to buy her a gold chain. He kept putting her off and avoided walking past any gold shops when he was with her. Eventually, just to shut her up, he said he would buy it next time he came back to Thailand. He was away for two months and forgot all about it. The very day he arrived back, she frogmarched him straight to a gold shop where she had obviously been eyeing off a nice necklace. He was then reminded of his 'promise' and shamed into coughing up the baht.

Of course, any promise made to you by a Pattaya Hostess is a different matter. You must remain patient and understanding if they fail to deliver on that promise, deny all knowledge of it or come up with the most elaborate excuse as to why they could not fulfil their obligation. Keep a smile on your face.

Lesson Seven – Face

Books about Asian culture often mention the concept of 'face'. If they don't, they should! Money may be the root of all evil but 'face' is the root of much of the negative or confusing behaviour displayed by many Asian people. To 'lose face' means a loss of respect, being shamed or looked down on by others while 'gaining face' means gaining prestige or status in the eyes of others. Do not underestimate the importance most Asians place on this. On occasions it is the reason behind any lies or aggression.

His wife got her driver's license. Seeing it was only three days between the time she applied and when the license was in her hands, he correctly assumed that she had not undergone any form of driver training or completed any recognized competency test. He bought her a cheap second-hand car as her introduction to mobile happiness.
After receiving her less than glowing gift, she was heard to say loudly in front of his friends, "My best friend have husband Denmark. She get license and after two days he buy her new car. My other best friend have husband Sweden. She have license one week then he buy her new car. I have husband Australia. Have license two weeks and he buy me Cheap Charlie old car. No good."

MONEY NUMBER ONE

"The number of concerned brothers visiting their sisters in Pattaya is only exceeded by the number of monoped fowls hopping along Beach Road."

NEIL HUTCHISON

The lady had lost face in front of her two best friends and nothing short of receiving the latest in road fashion would get it back.

> *"Oh Lord / won't you buy me / a Mercedes Benz;*
> *My friends all drive Porsches / I must make amends."*
> Janis Joplin

It has been reported that a few Pattaya Bar Hostesses play innocent and charming little 'face' games with their friends about their supposed wealth or social status. The 'my *farang* is better than your *farang*' game in particular, whereby she exaggerates the amount of money her *farang* boyfriend/husband earns and gives her, is all in the spirit of fun. However, the worst and potentially the most dangerous thing you can do to an Asian is be the cause of them losing face in front of their friends, even if it was unintentional on your part. Sometimes you may not even know you have done it.

> *Many Beer Bar complexes provide, for a small charge, a communal toilet for patrons and staff. After using the facilities, a farang came back to his friends and asked if the price for a pee had risen to 10 baht. They replied no, as the price written on the wall was still only 3 baht. The female toilet attendant had not given him change for his 10 baht coin so he went back to get it. (His resolve was due to the principle, not for the want of 7 baht.) He unwisely asked the attendant why she had tried to cheat him before he collected his 7 baht change and returned to the bar. Within two minutes, the attendant strutted over to where he was sitting and angrily shouted, for everyone to hear, that he could never use her toilet facilities again. Then she stormed off.*

That incident may seem trivial to Westerners but, when he accused her of trying to cheat him, she had 'lost face' even though nobody was around to see the exchange. When she came over and banned him from ever using her toilet again, there were many witnesses (especially Thai witnesses who understood her perfectly). By publicly asserting her authority over the impudent foreigner she had gained her 'face' back.

In Western society we place more importance on honesty and sincerity than 'face'. Some of us have so little 'face' it is hard to see our reflection in the mirror. Nevertheless, think of it this way: When your

Western wife or girlfriend asked you, "Honey, do you think I'm putting on weight?" you almost certainly replied something like, "No darling, you look as slim as they day we first met." You were probably thinking, "No darling, 52-inch hips and rolls of fat become you," but you lied to her in order to save her 'face' and your own miserable hide. Thais too, will lie and go to extraordinary lengths to save their own face or the face of someone who they consider to be a close friend or socially superior to themselves.

Lesson Eight – Aggression

Any time you mix alcohol with people of different cultures and backgrounds, there is bound to be some aggressive or violent behaviour. For a city its size, there is surprisingly very little visible violence in Pattaya involving tourists. Hopefully, the reason is that everybody is too busy having a good time to bother fighting each other. Whatever the reason, it is good news.

Looking at the stories behind the violence reported in the press or depicted on television news, most is not the result of random acts. It is usually infighting amongst criminals, a pre-planned assault, gangland brawling, jealous rage over a wife/girlfriend, a business or domestic dispute or a simmering tribal feud finally exploding.

As a foreign guest in the country, you should avoid violence at all costs. If you do happen to witness an altercation, stay out of it. This is particularly true if the fight or argument involves Thai people. Thais are very caring, placid and gentle people, however they can snap in a second and their anger knows no bounds. They act without considering the consequences of their actions and it can get deadly serious. Even if your girlfriend is involved in a foray with other Thais, stay out of it. Don't try and be John Wayne or attempt to act as peacemaker. You cannot win. Let the Thais sort it out, then be on hand with a band-aid, aspirin and comforting shoulder should your ladylove require it. In general, any time you encounter a problem, walk away. If the problem is very serious, seek out the Tourist Police and let them handle it.

To limit even the possibility of confrontation, the less you have to do with local Thai males, the better. Unless you know them very well, you should not accept gifts, food or drink from anyone. Politely refuse any unsolicited offers of advice, suggestions or help and avoid doing anything which could make them angry. Because alcohol can bring out the worst in people, never go out on a drinking spree with, pursue an argument with or attempt to 'get tough' with a Thai man. Many a foreigner has thought he has won an altercation and settled it, only to find that the guy returns later with a few of his friends to even the score. As noted in the previous lesson, it is all a matter of 'losing face' which means less to us than it does to them. It is far better to grin and bear it, apologise and walk away than end up in hospital, or worse.

Lesson Nine – Sentimentality

The practicalities of daily survival mean that Thais are generally not very sentimental. They can't afford to be. To many, if they can't spend it, sell it, eat it, wear it, live in it or ride it, they don't want it.

You may wish to prove your love and devotion by giving your Thai girlfriend or wife that 100-year-old copper brooch your great grandmother gave you on her deathbed, but the gesture will be totally lost on her. Why? Because the world copper price is low. If it were gold, however, it would be a different story. Forgetting about its historical or sentimental value, in times of need it could be sold for the weight of the gold. Souvenirs, keepsakes and mementos are equally as meaningless unless, of course, they are made of gold.

Any photos of previous girlfriends you may keep for purely sentimental reasons, whether they are printed or stored on your camera, phone or in your computer, should be hidden away from, and never shown to, your current flame. She will not understand your desire to keep them.

> *The guy came back to his apartment to find his live-in girlfriend sitting on the side of their bed with a trash can in front of her. When he got closer, he noticed she was tearing up photos she had removed from his photo album. Every photo he had taken with another lady was now in little pieces. When he became angry, she simply told him he didn't need them anymore now that he had her.*

Similarly, if she allows you to see her photo album, it will contain many 'half photos', i.e. photos in which she appears but the other person has been deftly removed with a pair of scissors.

Nowadays, with the proliferation of mobile phone cameras, most photos are digital so it is very easy to hit the 'delete' button. Western men who have had failed relationships with Asian ladies report that every photo of the two of them together lasted only as long as they did. Immediately after breaking up, the foreigner's image was cut out or the digital image was deleted. Letters, e-mails were similarly disposed of and the good times they may have had together were forgotten.

Lesson Ten – Here and Now

Many people throughout the world tend to live from moment to moment, one day at a time. They don't think about the future and short-term gain is preferable to future promises. To put it another way, 'a bird in the hand is worth two in the bush'. You will meet many such people while enjoying your visit to Thailand, so remember that they will not put too much faith in what you say you *will* do or what you say you *will* deliver sometime down the track. What is more important to them is what you are doing and delivering *now*.

Similarly, the past is usually forgotten quickly, especially any financial help you may have provided, any favour you have granted or kindness you have shown. Male visitors would be wise to heed the words of Marcus Antonius: *"The evil that men do lives after them; the good is oft interred with their bones."*

Lesson Eleven – Borrowing

Visitors to Pattaya can be excused for believing that the Thai word for 'borrow' has exactly the same meaning as the word 'give'. Don't expect anything borrowed from you to be returned and asking for it back is simply too rude to contemplate, besides being a total waste of time and effort.

> *The foreigner loaned the lady 3,000 baht to help her out of trouble, with her promise she would return it at the end of the month. Two months later, he politely asked her for the money back. She became all flustered and walked away. His girlfriend, the lady's friend, subsequently derided him for asking for the money back because, as she explained, her friend was 'shy'.*

The rule is simple: If you can't afford to lose it, don't lend it. That applies to lending to foreigners in Pattaya as well. Many Bar Girls borrow money from their friends just before leaving town. It goes without saying that local Bar Hostesses have a deserved reputation in so far as executing their obligation to the repayment of debts.

Lesson Twelve - Drinking

Thai beer is, of course, the best in the world and Thai whisky is regarded in jealous awe by Scottish distillers. It is no wonder many Thai people are so fond of it. Nevertheless, many Bar Hostesses refrain from intoxicants, preferring to keep their minds as sharp and alert as possible at all times.

Unfortunately, like the rest of the human race, some Thai imbibers can become aggressive when drunk so visitors should always be careful when drinking with a group of locals. Parties can last all night with booze disappearing faster than last month's pay packet. It will only stop when they run out of alcohol, run out of money to buy more alcohol or they collapse into unconsciousness. Should one innocent comment or 'look' on your part be felt inappropriate by an inebriated guest, the scene could get nasty.

Lesson Thirteen - Eating

Exotic, delicious Thai food is justifiably worshipped around the world so it is easy to understand why Thai people seem to have a preoccupation with eating. Whenever they feel hungry, eating is the most important thing on their mind. While Westerners usually eat three relatively substantial meals a day, a Thai will eat smaller meals up to eight times a day. Dieticians tell us eating smaller portions whenever you feel hungry is actually a healthy way of life. Compare the number of fat *farang* you see in Pattaya to the number of overweight Thais.

Eating is a social event for Thais, something to be shared with friends and family. To be seen eating alone may be an indication that you have no friends while to eat in front of others without offering to share your meal is considered bad manners. This is why Thai people will always offer you their food. If you know them well, it would be impolite to refuse. Even if you are not hungry and try only a mouthful, they will appreciate your gesture.

MONEY NUMBER ONE

The guy was raised to never waste food. At his girlfriend's home up country, he ate everything on his plate and thanked her parents gratiously. He was handed another plate of food and, even though he was full, did not wish to appear impolite. He finished that and another plate was put in front of him. He finally had to give up as he could not fit another mouthful. His girlfriend explained to him later that, because he ate everything on the plate, they thought he was still hungry. Eventually, they ran out of food and sent someone up to the shop to buy some more.

Lesson Fourteen - Taboos

Thai society is extremely hierarchical and everything, including people, assume a 'rank' relative to others within the group. From the book *Thailand Fever*:

"Even body parts are accorded ranks. The highest part of the body, the head, is considered the most sacred part, and Thais are uneasy if you touch their head or sit on a pillow meant for the head."

Many foreigners have the endearing habit of patting or stroking the head of their Thai lady. She will usually pass it off and not show any degree of discomfort at this behaviour but, below the surface, your action will be less than appreciated. Note that, should a Thai person need to touch your head, he or she will often excuse themselves before doing so: *"Kor toht ka/krap."*

"The lowest parts, the feet, are considered base and it is very offensive to point at objects or people with them."

You should never point with your feet or pick something up with your toes. Apart from that, in Pattaya, European influence is such that they do not seem to worry about 'the feet thing' too much so there is no need to be constantly on your guard for fear of accidentally offending someone. *Mai bpen rai!* [Don't worry about it].

It has been said that Thais do not like the colour black because of its association with death. Hah! More people are wandering around Pattaya wearing black outfits than at a Sicilian funeral. Black jeans, black t-shirts, black skirts, black dresses. Check it out.

Finally, it has been said there is a taboo about getting your hair cut on a Wednesday. Apparently, Thais won't cut hair or get a haircut on Wednesday for some reason. What a load of rubbish! You can get a haircut any day of the week.

Lesson Fifteen - Sleeping

An amusing article in the *Bangkok Post* suggested that you know you have been in Thailand too long when you can sleep standing up on a bus. This is true, as many witnesses can attest. The hard-working Thai people can do with little or no sleep for long periods but, when the need or opportunity arises, it appears they are capable of sleeping anywhere – in a thumping disco, on the side of a busy road or standing up in a bus. Seeing a Thai motorcycle taxi driver stretched out sound asleep on the back of his parked bike leaves many foreign visitors in awe of his skill and grace.

Some foreign men in Pattaya report their Thai ladylove is so fond of sleeping she can sleep sixteen hours a day if circumstances allow. When you stop and think about it, is it such a bad thing? Remember, while your wife or girlfriend is sleeping, she is not out spending (your) money. Bemoaning the fact she is either watching TV, eating or sleeping makes little sense when you consider that at least they are inexpensive habits. If she was either shopping, bingeing or whinging you would have more cause for concern.

Lesson Sixteen – Asking Directions

One problem consistent throughout Asia is that of obtaining accurate directions from locals. Of course, in Thailand, local people are only too eager to be courteous and helpful, and their knowledge of geography is unparalleled. (For confirmation of this, simply ask any foreign long-term resident of Pattaya.) Any misdirection can only be due to the foreigner's ignorance of the beautiful Thai language and his probable mispronunciation of place names. For example, the south eastern town of Trat is pronounced 'tart' as in 'custard tart'.

It is better to be self-reliant. Remember that many Asians believe answering a question by saying, "I don't know", when they could reasonably be expected to know the answer, means the other person may think they are less than intelligent and result in them losing face. To avoid this, they will sometimes give an answer - any answer - even if it is just a guess and totally inaccurate. By the time you find out the information was wrong, it is too late.

The guy was driving his girlfriend and her friend up country when he became lost. Wanting to save time, when he saw a policeman standing beside the road, he pulled over and told the very reluctant girls to get out and ask for directions. They

MONEY NUMBER ONE

finally did so and he guessed that they were chatting away with the policeman for at least fifteen minutes before returning to the car. They both nodded enthusiastically when he asked them if they now knew where to go.
He drove off and as they approached the next intersection asked, "Which way then?"
In unison, one girl pointed to the left and the other to the right.

Most signposts on major roads are written in Thai and English and highways are numbered, so study a map before you travel. Accurate maps can be purchased or found on the Internet but even the less detailed maps provided in free brochures and magazines can be of benefit for intercity journeys. Then you don't have to embarrass yourself or lose face by asking a local for directions to your place of interest.

Lesson Seventeen – Taking Photos

Be careful if you wish to take photos in and around the adult entertainment areas. As with casinos throughout the world, taking photos inside Go Go Bars is almost always prohibited so don't even take your camera inside. Some bars actually have security staff at the door to check so, if they ask for your camera, do the right thing and hand it over to them for safekeeping.

Taking photos in public areas or other places of entertainment is generally OK, but it is advisable to ask permission before happily snapping away. Always ask permission before taking photos of individual ladies or foreigners, for that matter. Most Thai ladies enjoy having their photo taken and will be only too happy to pose for you, but there may be the occasional one who, for whatever personal reason, does not appreciate it. In this digital age, many fear, with valid reason, that their photo may end up on the Internet.

Mike had only been in Pattaya for a couple of days and had not been warned about this. Drinking at a beer bar one evening, he innocently snapped a photo of an artificially-attractive silicon-enhanced woman who took immediate objection to it. She stormed off and reported the incident to her mentally-challenged foreign boyfriend who made his way towards Mike and told him, in no uncertain terms, what he would do to Mike and his camera if he took another photo of his girlfriend. Mike apologised, then, with knuckles dragging along the ground, the Neanderthal boyfriend slithered back into his cave.

Lesson Eighteen – *Wai*-ing

The custom of the *wai* - clasping the hands as if in prayer and bowing of the head - is common throughout Thailand, Laos, Burma and Cambodia. It is a very complex procedure. Depending on who *wais* first, where your hands are placed in relation to your head and how low your head is bowed, it can convey many levels of politeness and respect. Some foreign tourists show a lack of understanding of this and go about *wai*-ing willy-nilly every Asian person they come across, thinking it is 'cute'.

Without going into too much detail, you should only *wai* first to a person older than you, higher in social standing than yourself or someone to whom you wish to show deep respect. Examples are monks, Thai officials carrying guns and wearing uniforms emblazoned with campaign medals and epaulettes covered in gold stars (NOT the carpark attendant!), elected officials, doctors, teachers or anyone to whom you need to offer a sincere apology. You should never *wai* first to children, your wife or girlfriend, motorcycle taxi drivers, waiters, waitresses or Bar Hostesses, although you may politely return their *wai* if you wish.

One notable exception is that you should *wai* first when meeting your girlfriend's parents even though, in all likelihood, you will be older than them. This is a show of respect rather than relative age. And you don't have to *wai* them every time they appear; only as a first greeting and when you are saying goodbye.

Lesson Nineteen – Language

Many tourist guidebooks and books on Thai culture report that Thai people appreciate a foreigner who attempts to learn and speak their language and your efforts will make a good impression. This is true in most cases but, unfortunately, some Bar Hostesses do not appear to share this view. Yes, they know their language is difficult to learn but THAT IS THE WAY THEY LIKE IT! To them it is akin to a secret code which they can speak amongst themselves and foreigners will not have a clue what they are saying.

Bar Hostesses treat foreign men who can speak reasonable Thai differently to the 'mug' tourists. A foreigner going to the trouble of learning the language usually means he lives here or has visited often. In the first case, he probably has a Thai wife or at least a long-term girlfriend. In the

MONEY NUMBER ONE

second case, he may not have a Thai wife but he might have one or two girlfriends around. In both circumstances, it usually means the guy is familiar with the place and therefore he, "knows too much". (That is the exact translation of comments made by Bar Hostesses about such guys.)

It may even mean he has come to the bars simply to 'chill out' or maybe to 'butterfly' a little. The chances of a Bar Hostess extracting a large sum of money from him are not as good as if he were say, a run-of-the-mill tourist.

> *One Pattaya Bar Hostess told him all the ladies working in her bar liked him because he could speak Thai. Perhaps the fact he spoke Thai very badly (imagine Jed Clampett reciting Hamlet), meant the ladies were more amused than impressed.*

Even though they may no longer treat him as if he were a source of revenue and may drop many of the feminine charms reserved for the punters, this is not to say the Bar Hostesses would not go with a foreigner who can speak Thai. On the contrary. It is probably a relief for them because they know they can at least have a conversation, they don't have to be on their 'best' behaviour, they don't have to lie (but they will anyway) and they are still going to be paid for their time.

If you do learn to speak Thai, it is much more fun if you don't let on. Some of the conversation between Bar Hostesses is interesting when they think you cannot understand. Mostly though, their banter is very mundane. It is usually about brain surgery, Quantum Mechanics, the NASA Space Program or food. Like many women throughout the world, they can talk for hours about what they had to eat, what they are going to eat or what they would like to eat. Boring stuff.

> *One amusing trick is to go to a bar you have never been to before and pretend it is your first trip to Thailand, you just arrived and are staying for ten days. Any Bar Hostess with dollar signs in her eyes will swoop on that bait.*
> *One cunning linguist who did this in spite of his reluctance to relate an untruth to a wonderful Thai Hostess, recounted she could not speak a word of English and continually asked the mamasan what to do, how she could ask him to buy her a drink and how much she could request should he succumb to her more than worthy charms. He played totally dumb until,*

just before leaving, he answered all her questions in his best Thai.

Although the Thai spirit of fun is praiseworthy and he was sure they were only kidding, he felt nervous about ever returning to that particular bar.

It is strongly recommended that you learn at least the basics of the language if you plan to spend a lot of time in Thailand. There are many excellent books on the subject. There are a number of regional variations on the Thai language and Lao is widely spoken, but it is the tonal nature of the language which makes it extremely difficult for foreigners to learn. As an example, politely ask a Thai to read the following sentence and then try to repeat what you heard.

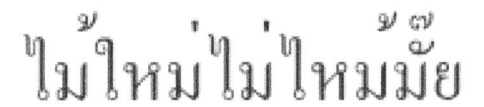

ไม้ใหม่ไม่ไหมมั้ย

In English it means, "New wood doesn't burn, does it?"

MONEY NUMBER ONE

5
Adult Fun & Entertainment

Various experts, expats and exiles suggest there are between 500 and 3,000 entertainment venues of all descriptions in Pattaya. It is highly likely that the '500 group' missed quite a few streets, while the latter group probably started seeing double after a few hours of research. One thing is for certain - the number fluctuates by the minute.

Basically, there are three types of Adult entertainment venues in Pattaya - Go Go Bars, Indoor Recreational Lounges (a.k.a. 'Short Time Bars') and Beer Bars. This book is deliberately not going to mention any particular bar by name nor make any recommendations. This is for three reasons. Firstly, the appeal of a bar depends on your own particular tastes. What one person finds appealing about one establishment may turn someone else off and vice versa. Secondly, bars open, close and change hands on a regular basis. Here today - gone tomorrow. Thirdly, the quality of a bar is highly dependent upon the staff working there. Bar Hostesses are free to come and go as they please and the high turnover of staff is always a problem for bar owners.

For example, you may enjoy drinking at a particular bar because of the wonderful ladies working there, only to return a month later to find the friendly, gorgeous little angels who stole your heart have scattered. They have been replaced by a bunch of nose-picking Noras that you would not give ten *baht* for, let alone pay a bar fine.

A 'tab' system operates at almost all places of adult entertainment in Pattaya, the exceptions being some discos and nightclubs. Each time you buy a drink, a docket is placed in a plastic or wooden cup in front of you. This is called your *'bin'*. When you decide to leave the bar, you merely have to say *'check bin'*. The dockets will be added up by the cashier and stapled together. The total should be written on the back and shown to you for payment.

TIP

Before you 'check bin' at a bar, always count up the bill yourself. This is not to say that the bars will try and cheat you, but it is much better to be safe than sorry. It has happened on several occasions that the customer has found the actual bill was 100 baht lower than the one quoted. He put this down to the girls' lack of higher education in mathematics. For collectors of statistics, it is surprising that all mistakes seem to be in the bar's favour. Even if you are so drunk that you don't know which way is 'up', at least be seen to be adding up the bill. You should have no problem thereafter.

Some bars in other parts of the world, for example in the Philippines, require the customer to sign each docket before it is placed in his bin. That way, he supposedly knows exactly how much he is being charged each time. This is not the case in Pattaya.

A foreign bar-owner attempted to start the practice at his bar. His Thai bar manager immediately shot down the idea by explaining that it meant each girl would have to carry a pen around with her. Too difficult. The owner agreed once he realized just how many pens they would lose each night.

MONEY NUMBER ONE

Some time ago, a bar did actually try this system. One customer had a long session one night and, since he was well known at this particular bar, put off paying his bill until the following day. (Not recommended practice.)
The next day he was astounded to find that his bill came to over 3,000 baht. He complained and, going through each docket with the bar manager, pointed out that some dockets carried a signature that was definitely not his own. "Yes," said the bar manager, "but you were very mao *[drunk] last night so I sign for you."*

You may notice that almost every place of entertainment in Pattaya has a bell hanging in a prominent position. This is NOT to call for service even though if you did ring it you would get the best and fastest service you have ever seen. It should only be rung if you are feeling very generous and your wallet is weighing you down. 'Ringing the bell' means that you have just shouted a drink for everyone in the bar, including all the hard-working staff. The Hostesses will go crazy with joy, your popularity will soar and your finances will shrink. Don't even think about ringing the bell in jest because it will not be taken as a joke.

A currently enforced ordinance requires all Pattaya bars to close by 1:00am but this curfew is continually under review and may increase to 2:00am or 3:00am during High Season. The minimum legal age to be served in a bar is 20 and the minimum age to be working behind a bar is 18. Prostitution is illegal and it is gratifying to read that foreign investigators, after several weeks of extensive research here, universally report they found no evidence to suggest any such immoral activity exists in Pattaya.

The fine line is that, due to the flexible nature of their working conditions, most - but not all - of the Hostesses employed in the bar will be allowed to leave with you upon your payment of her 'bar fine'. This amount, which varies depending on the type of bar and the season, is to compensate the bar for the lady's wages and the loss of her invaluable, conscientious services, whether it be for merely an hour or a full day. You may be asked to pay the bar fine seperately or a '*bin*' will be written out to be paid along with your drink tab once you '*check bin*'.

There are specific exceptions but, unlike parts of the Philippines and Cambodia, this bar fine DOES NOT include any fee the Hostess may impose for her personal time. That should be negotiated directly with the lady and NEVER paid in advance.

TIP
Before you and one or two friends bar fine Hostesses from the same bar, agree beforehand how much you will give each lady. They will certainly compare notes later so, if one received 500 baht, one 1,000 baht and one 1,500 baht, it makes the guy who paid the least look bad and the one who paid the most look stupid. The girl who received the least will have lost face.

Go Go Bars

These are the bars behind closed doors or heavy curtains, variously described as 'Ogling Dens' or 'Chrome-pole Palaces'. They often go by very quaint, imaginative and provocative names. In Pattaya, most Go Go Bars don't open until after 7:00pm and can be found in and around Walking Street, South Pattaya. A few scattered throughout the city open as early as 1:00pm. Some proudly advertise 'No Cover Charge' but, in truth, none actually impose a cover charge unless they are hosting a special occasion. For the privacy and comfort of their patrons, unescorted ladies and hawkers are usually not welcome in Go Go Bars.

> *Note that tourists from the Sub-continent and its surrounds have a poor reputation with bar owners. They are accused of going into bars as a group and only ordering one (the cheapest) drink between them. They sit and ogle the ladies for an hour or so before checking bin and leaving no tip. To discourage this behaviour, some bars impose an arbitrary Cover Charge on these easily-identified people. My friend and I squeezed past two such people arguing with the doorman who was charging them 100 baht each to enter. When they complained as to why we were let in without paying, he simply replied, "Regular customers."*

Inside the dimly lit decor, the impressive performers dress scantily and 'dance' around a series of chrome poles on a prominent stage. They usually wear a number attached to their clothing, but if clothing is limited, it may be on one of their shoes. Should an exquisite dancer take your fancy and you would like her to sit with you, it is simply a matter of pointing her out or quoting her number to a drink attendant. Most of the time though, all you have to do is smile at her. The dancers are not as shy as their sisters in

MONEY NUMBER ONE

the outdoor Beer Bars and some can be very forthright as to how they would like to please and entertain you, so be prepared. Some can also be very demanding when it comes to wanting you to buy them a 'lady drink'.

Some Go Go Bars provide provocative shows during which one or more entertainers will perform specialized 'acts' which cannot be described in these pages. Be assured they require a degree of sexual agility. The practice of some Go Go Bars providing 'short-time' rooms for customers and dancers to get better acquainted is illegal, therefore the rooms no longer exist. But if you don't believe that, then the bar fine for a private in-house game of Space Invaders will be between 300 and 600 *baht*. To take a dancer away as your overnight guest, the bar fine can be anywhere between 500 *baht* and 1,000 *baht*. The personal compensation for the lady's time spent with you starts from 700 *baht* for a 'short time' and from 1,200 *baht* for overnight.

Having said that, most Go Go Bars and their first-rate Hostesses and quality dancers increase their prices during high season. It is not simply a matter of 'supply and demand'. Firstly, owners want to discourage punters from running off with the bar's star attractions. They make their money from selling booze and an empty stage is not going to entice potential customers to sit down for a drink. Secondly, some Go Go dancers suddenly decide they are superstars by demanding 2,000 to 4,000 *baht* from cashed-up holidaymakers for their private companionship. Why? Because some men are stupid enough to pay it.

Displayed on the wall in some of the longer established Go Go Bars, an 'Honour Roll' contains the names of the punters credited with the most bell rings or horn blows. Maybe it is the guy who bought the most lady drinks, paid the most bar fines in a single day or holds some other dubious distinction. To be immortalized on a bar's 'Dickhead List' simply requires a minimum of brains and a maximum of *baht*.

> *I confess to once being on a 'bell-ringers' honour board. The rule stated any person who rang the bell was entitled to have his name etched on the wall along with the date. It was a 'low season' Sunday, the doors had just opened, it was Happy Hour and there were four people in the bar including myself. The bell ring cost me slightly over 200 baht. After finding out, the bar owner amended the conditions to exclude Sundays and Happy Hours. Prick.*

MONEY NUMBER ONE

Should you attend a Go Go Bars shortly after opening time, you may witness an interesting ritual. One of the dancers will strip completely naked and walk around the stage three times carrying a glass of water in one hand and perhaps a phallic object in the other. While the remaining Hostesses rattle bin cups on tables, she will dip the phallus (or fingers) into the water and sprinkle it over them all individually before finally tossing the remaining water between her legs and out onto the street. It is apparently performed as a good luck ceremony to attract customers to the bar and money to the girls, but there are doubts you will find it described in any books on Thai culture.

Indoor Recreation Lounges

Air-conditioned shophouse bars behind doors or curtains will have a few of their more attractive ladies sitting outside to entice customers off the street.

TIP

The thing I find annoying is that, in some cases, once the beautiful lady has gained your attention, taken your arm, escorted you inside, sat you down and asked what you would like to drink, she will deliver your drink and then promptly head back outside. You are left siting alone for the briefest of moments until one of the least attractive working ladies comes out of a dark corner and plants herself firmly beside you. Perhaps it is a good idea to ensure the good looking one outside understands your wish to be with her before you walk through the door.

There will probably not be any pole dancing but the Hostesses are definitely not shy. All are very friendly and obliging. The main attraction used to be that these bars provided rooms for patrons to go 'short time' with one of the Hostesses. If the mood overcame you, it was simply a matter of retiring to a private room with the apple of your eye in tow to enjoy a refreshing shower, engage in some light-hearted banter, perhaps play a video game or two, have another shower then return to the bar feeling rejuvenated. Of course, providing rooms for patrons to go 'short time' is illegal and therefore does not exist. That being said, many establishments take the law to be more of a suggestion than an ordinance, so don't be surprised if you find a bar more than accommodating in that area.

A 'short time' bar fine is around 300 *baht* which often includes the use of a private room on the premises. Most Hostesses employed in these establishments will accept the industry standard 700 *baht* for their personal services bringing the total impost to 1,000 *baht*. Nowadays some are initially demanding more so it is best to negotiate with the lady beforehand.

Like Go Go Bars, hawkers and unescorted ladies are not welcome inside these bars which are designed for the customer who, for one reason or another, wishes not to be seen in a bar. Many cold-hearted foreign men who already have a girlfriend, a wife, or both, visit these bars when they feel the need for the type of feminine companionship their wife/girlfriend would not understand.

The largest concentration of Indoor Recreation Lounges can be found in *Soi* 6 (a.k.a *Soi Yodsak*). A stroll down Soi 6 from mid-afternoon until late is truly an eye-opener.

Beer Bars

The majority of bars are Beer Bars which are spread across the city from Jomtien Beach in the south to Naklua in the north. The latest rough count indicates there are about 750 of these operational but new ones are constantly springing up while others are being abandoned. There seems to be no shortage of optimistic entrepreneurs eager to take up the challenge of running a bar. (More on that later in Chapter 12.) Beer Bars come in two basic designs: The kiosk and the shophouse.

The kiosk type, with gazebo-style roof and no walls, can be stand-alone or one of a cluster under one large roof. A communal toilet will be provided somewhere in the near vicinity but is usually not free. The charge is around five *baht*. That money is supposedly used for the upkeep and maintenance of the facilities but, at some places you could be forgiven for questioning where the money really goes.

Because of their open design these bars can never 'close' as such, always keeping at least one caretaker member of staff in attendance. To signify they are not open for business, the usual practice is to switch off the lights and music and upturn the bar stools. The real action takes place between 8:00pm and 1:00am when there could be up to thirty beautiful Bar Hostesses to serve you drinks, play games and keep you entertained. Most only cease serious activity once the last customer has left in the wee small hours.

MONEY NUMBER ONE

The shophouse type Beer Bars occupy one, two or three 4-metre-wide shophouses in the ground floor of buildings. Often providing budget accommodation on the floors above, they operate on the same principle as the kiosk type except the toilet is free and they may close at some point of the morning. A few may have a 'short time' room available, although this seems to be offered as a customer convenience rather than an income-generating business practice.

Some of the Beer Bars have live bands performing at night and some provide karaoke. (Note: If you cannot sing, do everyone a favour. Don't!) Some have pool tables, a dart board or big-screen TV to keep customers entertained. Even if you are alone and feel like a game of eight-ball, one of the Hostesses will be happy to play with you. After a game or two it would be polite, but not compulsory, to buy her a drink in appreciation for her time. If you like to play for money, do so at your own risk. It is surprising how a lady's game can dramatically improve once there is *baht* at stake.

Thais in Pattaya appear to be under the impression that loud music attracts foreign customers so every Beer Bar has at least a 30,000 watt stereo system and competes to see who can play the loudest noise. There is no problem playing Western music but, surprisingly, bar owners require a special licence to play Thai music. It supposedly has to do with paying royalties to Thai recording companies and some bars have been fined 30,000 *baht* and shut down for a month for the 'crime' of having a Thai music CD behind the bar. If you have ever heard any *Isaan* folk songs you may come to appreciate this quirky law.

TIP
If you do not like the Eagles' *song 'Hotel California', take earplugs with you. It would be difficult to spend a night in Pattaya without hearing this song. It is played to death.*

One disadvantage of drinking at a Beer Bar is that you can be harassed by hawkers selling everything from flowers, watches, copy Viagra, lottery tickets, clothing, a shoeshine to chewing gum and cigarettes. This is especially true if the bar is one of the kiosk type and close to the street. Many of the hawkers are children and can become annoying. Unless you desperately need something they are selling, it is best to politely refuse their offers. If something does take your fancy and you wish to do a bit of bargaining, the general rule is that the correct price is about one-third of their initial offer. If you get them down to around half the original asking price, you are doing OK.

NEIL HUTCHISON

The farang jokingly asked a copywatch salesman if he had a copy Timex or copy Casio. The hawker smiled "no" and the farang laughed. The following evening at the bar, the same hawker came up to the farang and produced one ladies and one gents Timex copywatch from his bag. The astonished farang was shamed into a purchase.

The problem is exacerbated when a foreign tourist does actually buy something from one of the vendors. World satellite communication systems have got nothing on the hawker sales network.

A farang with a 'good heart' bought a few bunches of flowers for some of his female admirers. Within milliseconds, word had spread to every flower vendor within running distance. The bar resembled the opening Covent Garden scene from My Fair Lady. Eventually the ever-helpful mamasan came to his rescue and dispersed the zealous throng.

The Games People Play

There are four main games that the Bar Hostesses enjoy playing at the bar. These are used to relieve boredom (both yours and theirs) due to your communication problems, to keep you amused and to keep you drinking at the bar. The clever Hostesses often play these games amongst themselves during slack times when there are no *farang* about.

The most common game is played with dice. It comprises a wooden box with the numbers 1 to 9 painted on wooden flippers and two dice. You throw the dice and, depending on what you throw, flip over one of the wooden numbers. e.g. If you throw a 1 and a 4, then you can turn either the 1, the 4, or a combination of both, 5. If the numbers you throw have already been taken, your turn is over. The idea is to clear all the numbers and sometimes it can take many games before someone wins. Although it is purely a game of chance, Bar Hostesses who have been in Pattaya a long time become experts at this game.

TIP
You do not have to be a mathematical genius to work out the probabilities of throwing a particular number. The idea is to

MONEY NUMBER ONE

work from the outside in. Leave the 5 and the 6 until last. The chances of throwing a particular number increase in the following order: 9-8-7-1-2-3-4-5-6.

The second game is 'Bingo Line-up' or 'Connect 4', a game consisting of a vertical plastic frame down which you drop coloured tokens in turn. The purpose is to get 4 of your tokens together in a row (vertically, horizontally or diagonally) while stopping your opponent from doing likewise. Unlike the dice game, this is a game of skill. Bar Hostesses who play this game for hours each and every day become very good at it and they enjoy the challenge and thrill of victory. No hints can be offered on how to win at this game.

The next game is 'Jenga'. It consists of a tower of wooden blocks arranged in a hatch formation. The idea is, using only one hand, to take a block from somewhere within the stack and place it on top, thus building the tower higher. If the tower falls during your turn, you lose. This is a game of skill requiring a steady hand. It should not be played after consuming twelve beers or when you are sitting directly in the path of a fan. The beautiful, agile Bar Hostesses are very good at playing this game too.

The last game is dominos and every bar will have a set or two. The game is played under local rules which differ from bar to bar so if you are keen to play get acquainted with all the rules first.

This is a fictitious story about a fictitious farang who played dominos with three fictitious Bar Hostesses at a fictitious bar in a fictitious soi. The farang lost 800 baht playing for 20 baht per game. Doing the math, that is a losing streak of forty games! Was he a born loser, or was there something more sinister afoot?

These games may all seem a bit childish, but what the hell. You are here on holiday, they are harmless fun and great icebreakers. The true purpose of playing is not to win, but to fill in time between slurps of cold beer and to get better acquainted with your charming opponent.

TIP
After you have played a few games with a charming, beautiful Hostess, and if you enjoy her company, it is polite to offer to buy her a drink. After all, she is entertaining you when she possibly could be eating or gossiping with her friends. Once you have bought her a drink, she will most likely be happy to continue toying with you as long as you want.

TIP
Although gambling is illegal in Thailand, before playing any game with a gorgeous Hostess for money, make sure she actually has the money, in the remote possibility that you win. Don't just ask her and wait for her to say "yes". Ask to actually see the cash. Many years ago, a certain farang was owed a lot of money by a lot of little angels because he did not check their financial status before playing games for money. You know, 20 baht here, 40 baht there. It all adds up. In spite of emphatic promises from award-winning actresses, he had more chance of winning the Thai lottery than ever collecting the debts.
The rule is simple: If the farang loses, he must pay up immediately. If she loses, it is on the 'never-never' system.

Gambling

Apart from the Government-run lottery and the few horse racing tracks around the country, gambling is strictly illegal in Thailand. Two very well maintained horse racing tracks are located in Bangkok and meetings are held each Sunday, alternating between the two venues.

The National Lottery is held (usually) on the 1st and 16th of each month and tickets go on sale about a week or so before the draw. The price of a ticket (two half-shares) is 100 *baht* from a street stall but vendors walking around carrying wooden cases loaded with lottery tickets will charge you 110 *baht*. The lowest prize dividend is 1,000 *baht*, but there is a 3% (30 *baht*) tax so you will only receive 970 *baht* (full ticket 1,940 *baht*) when you collect. The excruciatingly long and complicated lottery draw is held live on television during the afternoon and if you are a total masochist, watch it.

MONEY NUMBER ONE

As far as can be ascertained, even playing the game of dominos is illegal. Perhaps the authorities realize that most Thais are not likely to be playing the game just for fun. When the Bar Hostesses play amongst themselves, the domino tiles may be hidden behind the bar, well out of view. When the police raid an evil domino game, the participants are rounded up, taken to the policestation, have the domino tiles and any money on their person confiscated and fined around 100 *baht* each.

Should the Hostesses be playing dominos or cards with a *farang*, the police will (usually) turn a blind eye. They intelligently realize that foreigners may not be aware of the law and, in the spirit of tourism, will not (usually) react if they spot the evil tiles or cards in the hands of a foreigner. No money should be visible or seen to be changing hands so keep any money out of sight at all times. There was at least one case in 2011 where two foreign males were apprehended for playing dominos and were each given a 1,000 *baht* fine. That's ten times the Thai rate.

An interesting article appeared in *Pattaya Trader* magazine of July 2005 in which a Police Colonel attempted to explain the law on playing cards:

"Gambling is illegal in Thailand but people can still play cards in public areas, so long as they are not playing for money or property. In fact, people often play cards at the airport while waiting for a flight. People may play cards for forfeits, such as taking off their clothes or drinking or whatever, that is not a problem, but it is if there is money or property involved.

"Of course, even if we cannot see money changing hands during a game, we cannot be sure that the players aren't playing for money or something similar - such as meals or goods, for example.

"If a police officer cannot be sure that people are not playing for money or similar, he must stop them playing. If we don't do this we could end up with locals and tourists gambling all over the place. The reason why playing cards are sold so widely here is because there are still many people who use them for telling fortunes; they don't buy them for gambling."

Doesn't it all make sense now it has been explained to you?

There is a fascinating angle to the card playing ban. It is perfectly legal to play cards and gamble to your heart's content - at a Thai funeral. Inside the Wat grounds, presumably near the coffin of the dearly departed, friends and relatives can (and do) conduct marathon card playing and gambling sessions to keep the spirit of the departed company while he/she moves to the next incarnation. And the police won't interfere. This could explain why Thai funerals are often well-attended.

Massages

You cannot say you have been to Thailand until you have tried a Thai massage. The genuine ones (i.e. no sexual contact) are extremely relaxing and great for all your aches, pains and hangovers.

Foot massages (from 100 *baht*/hour) are excellent for soothing tired, aching feet. Oil massages and Body Scrubs are popular and plentiful. They are relatively inexpensive, starting at around 200 *baht* per hour. Scalp massages, head massages and aromatherapy are also popular with tourists.

An oil massage at around 300 *baht* per hour sometimes offers the opportunity for an optional 'extra' whereby the girl uses oil and her hands to relieve your most intimate tensions. This is known as a 'Happy Ending'. She will naturally ask for additional money for this service and, when you ask how much extra, she may use the industry standard response of, "Up to you!" In general, you will get away with 200 *baht* which, when added to the cost of the massage, makes it a convenient 500 *baht* total.

Full body massages are not difficult to find. Euphemistically called 'white water rafting', 'soapy suds' or 'slippery slide', when you try it you will understand why. Inside the building, you will be greeted with the sight of an assortment of pretty, well dressed, smiling Thai Hostesses sitting on tiered seats behind a glass wall. You can sit at a table or lounge chair, order a drink, relax and watch the ladies as they give you their best 'come on' looks. Any time a girl takes your fancy, simply tell a waiter her number (prominently displayed on her clothing) and she will come out and sit with you.

You can buy her a drink and the two of you can simply sit and chat for as long as the drink lasts or until she decides you are a waste of time. Should you wish to take the relationship further, a full body massage will cost you around 600 *baht* for ninety minutes. The girl's personal services are extra and negotiable. Costing a minimum of 1,000 *baht*, her first offer may be anywhere between 1,500 and 2,000 *baht*. At the time of writing, at least three of the better establishments in North Pattaya near Big C offer a 1,600 *baht* all-inclusive arrangement. This is a good deal even though some of the more experienced Hostess will still try it on for an additional 'tip' afterwards. Condoms are insisted upon.

Other Entertainment

It may surprise you to learn that, apart from the bars, there are other forms of entertainment in Pattaya. When the bars and girls get a bit too much for you, here are some alternatives:

1. Pool & Snooker
   Many bars, both indoor and outdoor, provide pool tables free of charge for their customers and operate under the 'challenge table' rules. For some bars, mainly those with the smaller American tables, the cost to play can be 10 or 20 *baht* per game. Be warned that the surface of some older tables would make Neil Armstrong feel right at home. There are also a number of air conditioned snooker halls throughout the city where quality tables and cues can be found, charging from around 100 *baht* per hour. If you cannot find an opponent, one of the staff will only be too happy to oblige. Most Thai people enjoy playing pool or snooker and some are very skilled.

2. Thai Boxing
   There are several Thai Boxing rings in Pattaya set among nests of Beer Bars. If you like Thai boxing, just sit at any of the bars nearby. The show is free to watch but the drinks are more expensive as each bar contributes to the cost of the shows. When their bout is finished, the boxers disperse into the crowd to solicit tips, almost exclusively from *farang*. Understand that these are exhibition bouts only and are about as genuine as those American TV wrestling shows. To see a genuine Thai Boxing tournament, ask at any tourist agency or look for details of the regular Friday night professional bouts held at the stadium on *Thepprasit* Road.

3. Live Sex Shows
   These are illegal and therefore do not exist, but if you stroll along Walking Street in South Pattaya any night of the week, you may be approached by touts advertising the shows. Be warned: No matter what you are told, NONE of them are actually free. Drink prices are invariably outrageous and the scams are notorious. Stay right away from out-of-the-way, dimly-lit, seedy areas!

4   Cabarets
Of all the professional, glitzy, glamorous cabaret and 'lady-man' shows in Pattaya, probably the most well known is Tiffany's Transvestite Cabaret Show which has been running for 30 years. There are three shows nightly at 18:00, 19:30 and 21:00. These 'extravaganzas' are very professional, have astonishing sets, dazzling costumes, a hefty cover charge and are very popular. For the less discerning, there are stages set up in or near some main bar areas which also offer cabaret-style entertainment. Most are free to watch but the drinks are a little more expensive.

In my opinion, the best of these is Malibu Show on Second Road at the corner with *Soi* 13/2 which has also been running for many years. Malibu shows are nowhere near as professional as Tiffany's but can be a lot of fun all the same. The 'Tina Turner' show is particularly popular. Sometimes the performers call for audience participation so shy people would be wise to sit up the back.

5   Discos
If you are deaf or own a good pair of ear plugs, you are welcome to go to one of the many discos around town. Oh, you will also need a large amount of cash. Most discos don't really get thumping and pumping until around midnight, have all the latest high-tech gear, play all the latest mindless noise and charge like there is no tomorrow. On the positive side, there is usually no shortage of ladies present since many freelancers make the clubs their happy hunting ground.

6   Movies
There are four cinema complexes in Pattaya. The newest is the SFX complex of nine theatres on the 6th (top) floor of Central Festival shopping mall between *Sois* 9 and 10. SFX offers four pricing deals every day (prices do not rise on weekends). 'Deluxe' is 120 *baht*, 'Premium' is 150 *baht*, 'Sofa' is 500 *baht* and 'First Class' is 600 *baht*. Not sure what the difference is.

Another is located in Big C shopping centre opposite *Soi* 2 on Second Road, while the Alangkarn complex on Sukhumvit Road at Jomtien is not easy to get to using public transport. Finally, the Major Cineplex can be found on Second Road opposite *Soi* 13. All venues show the latest Thai movies and foreign films with subtitles in Thai.

MONEY NUMBER ONE

7   Ten Pin Bowling

There are four Ten Pin Bowling alleys in town, all located on Second Road. One is above Tops Supermarket at the corner with Central Road, one in The Avenue Shopping Mall opposite *Soi* 13, one in the latest Central Festival shopping mall between *Soi* 10 and *Soi* 9 and another in North Pattaya opposite Big C shopping centre.

8   Go Kart and Motor Racing

If you wish to get some realistic driving practice before venturing onto Pattaya's streets, there are two Go Kart Speedway circuits on *Thepprasit* Road Jomtien and one off *Sukhumvit* Road in North Pattaya. There is also a small one off Naklua Road to the north of the city. A 2.4 kilometre International motor and motorcycle racing circuit (BIRA) is located not far from Pattaya for more serious speed junkies.

9   Golf

Apparently there are 17 world class golf courses within 30 minutes drive of Pattaya. Green fees and other charges are very reasonable compared to courses in the West. Many bars and hotels offer daily golfing outings which usually includes transportation, club and buggy hire for one all-inclusive price. Pattaya also has several Driving Ranges for those in need of swinging practice.

10   Shooting, Fishing, Sailing, Scuba Diving, Snorkelling, Windsurfing, Water Skiing, Sky Diving, Bungee Jumping

Plenty of opportunities so ask around for the best places and the best deals. Ocean swimmers should be aware the water off Pattaya is not as clean as it could be, so Koh Larn, the popular island off Pattaya Bay, are better alternatives. Pattaya Park, a large water amusement park situated between Pattaya and Jomtien, has water-slides and whirlpools.

Warning to anyone hiring jet skis. The jet ski operators are perhaps the biggest scam artists in the city. The thirty-minute hire will cost about 700 *baht* but - on many occasions - the operator will point to a scratch or dent on the machine when you return it. Whether you were responsible for the damage or it was already there, you will be charged an obscene amount of money for the repairs and often threatened with violence if you don't pay up.

11   Cultural Shows, Temples, Elephants, Tigers, Crocodiles, Botanical Gardens
       Yes.

MONEY NUMBER ONE

6
The Hostesses Employed in Pattaya's Adult Entertainment Industry

In spite of emphatic denials, the main attraction many foreign men find in Pattaya is the ladies. Not only are they fun-loving, friendly, happy and attractive, but they also have inner qualities which seem to strike at the very heart of foreign men. It is not just their eyes or their smile but their ability to say the right thing at the right time which can turn grown men into putty. A naked Go Go dancer on stage could give you such a look to have you believe she was as pure and innocent as the driven snow. They are experts at making visitors feel welcome and men feel like kings, and it would take a man of stone not to fall in love several times a day.

They are a paradox. On the one hand they will talk freely and openly about sex and the most intimate details of their lives yet, in the privacy of a bedroom, dress and undress with a towel around them because they are shy. Even the girls who work in Go Go Bars and display all or 99% of their bodies to ogling foreign customers can be shy in the bedroom. One minute they will tell you they don't like men who 'butterfly' and next week go with seven different customers in as many days. They will tell you that they do not like lies or people who tell lies and in the next breath come out with the biggest load of garbage you've ever heard. If Hollywood ever runs short of actresses, they should send their talent scouts to Pattaya.

Peter's girlfriend had a roommate, Lek, who had an English boyfriend, John. Lek worked in a beer bar but Peter was told she did not go with farang because she was waiting for John to return. When he eventually arrived in Pattaya, he booked a room next to Peter's. One night the two guys went on a 'boys only' bar crawl, during which John became enamoured with a cute Bar Hostess. At 2:00am Peter left John in the arms of the latest object of his desire. John's intention was to strike up a 'short-time' union with her.
Back at the apartment, Peter was confronted by Lek who asked where John was. Of course he lied, saying that he was drinking with some friends he had met and would be back soon.
At dawn, Peter was awakened by the sound of Lek crying. She was sitting on the floor looking at her photo of John and sobbing uncontrollably. He felt truly sorry for her. When John finally crawled back at about 7:00am, he managed to explain (lie) his way out of it.
The twist to this story is, after John left, Peter found out that Lek had another boyfriend, an American, who arrived a few days later. Both John and the American were sending her money. Like Peter, his girlfriend had lied to protect a friend and Lek had put on an Academy Award winning performance for his benefit.

But the question remains as to why a Thai lady would opt to work bar in the first place. Wouldn't she much rather be living with her family or husband and working at a 'respectable' job? The answer to the first question is blatantly obvious: for m-o-n-e-y. The answer to the second is: probably, but good husbands and 'respectable', well-paid jobs are hard to come by. Do her parents know what she does for a living? Probably. Do they care? Probably not. The economic benefits to her family far outweigh any moral concerns.

A few are truly desperate and see no other means of earning an income. Before condemning their actions, it should be remembered that to them, working in a bar and perhaps going with a customer for sex is just a job. Just as we would go to work each day in our own country, these ladies go to work

MONEY NUMBER ONE

in a bar. Certainly, some of them don't like the work. How many of us work at a job we hate but do it because it offers security, we have bills to pay or we simply cannot find a better career?

Working in a bar has its advantages. It is not difficult nor does it require any particular skill or educational qualification. Work opportunities are so plentiful that, in most cases, the lady simply has to turn up at a bar and say she wants a job. She then has the potential to earn a lot of money, the opportunity to sleep most of the day and, if she is so inclined, to party most of the night.

Some do it for a limited time for a specific purpose; to buy a motorbike, pay for education, pay off a debt etc. Once that goal has been achieved, they quit just as easily as they started.

Others do it because the money they have the potential to earn is just too good to pass up. There are a significant number of ladies in Pattaya earning more than 100,000 *baht* per month. To put that in perspective: the average monthly *household* income in the northeast areas of Thailand from which most of these girls originate is just over 10,000 *baht*; a recent poll found that 76% of the Thai population earn less than 15,000 *baht* per month; and 15,000 *baht* has been *proposed* as the minimum wage for people holding a university degree.

Then there are a small number who do it for the more express purpose of finding a foreign husband because, rightly or wrongly, they have heard that Western men treat and take care of women better than Thai men. The chances of her finding a potential foreign boyfriend or husband wandering around her village is remote.

"However, at the end of the day, they're still well aware of their status in Thai society ...

"Bar girls may feel like a stained cloth in Thai eyes: now that it's publicly known that they've slept with a lot of men, they assume that no Thai man would ever marry them, or that any Thai they're with would look down on them. This may reinforce the idea that a Westerner is their only way out ..."

Thailand Fever, by Chris Pirazzi & Vitida Vasant

An interesting article appeared in a Thai magazine reporting that in Isaan (pronounced *'ee-sarn'*, it is the large area comprising the north east and central east of Thailand), it is the 'fashion' (exact translation) for young ladies to have a *farang* boyfriend. Whether that boyfriend is a status symbol to be worn on the arm like a trophy, for the lady, he is a means to an end.

NEIL HUTCHISON

Finally, there are the ladies who take to bar work like a duck to water. Their initial reasons for working in the industry are lost amidst the hedonistic, party atmosphere. They learn to enjoy the lifestyle, the money and, dare we say it, the sex. When their physical attriveness wanes over time, some stay on in the business as *mamasans* or even become bar owners themselves.

Whatever her motives, she has not been sold into 'sexual slavery' nor has she been forced at gunpoint to work in the bars. Although this type of abomination does exist in Southeast Asia, it is usually contained in areas away from the eyes of the foreign press. It is certainly not present in Pattaya bars catering to foreigners. A Pattaya Bar Hostess is free to quit at any time but, if she chooses to stay, it is most often because the economic benefits far outweigh anything else on offer.

"People ... think that all prostitutes are virtual slaves in their occupation, and that they would instantly jump ship if they could get a job washing dishes or cleaning houses. However, many of these women actually left such jobs to work in the higher-paying sex industry, and then stayed in the sex industry for ten years or more.

"...despite the difficulties and risks, 70,000 - 300,000 women [in Thailand] *have decided that the sex industry is their best option."*

Thailand Fever, by Chris Pirazzi & Vitida Vasant

Bangkok 8, by John Burdett offers another fascinating insight into the mind-set of Thai sex workers. The following is particularly revealing:

"These days a huge percentage of young women studying at university and colleges are subsidized by so-called sugar daddies - men, often farangs but usually Thai, who pay their expenses, even a kind of salary, in exchange for the right to sleep with the students whenever they choose. It is not illegal, but the girl is certainly selling her body. If the sugar daddy isn't rich enough to pay all her expenses, she'll have to take on another, perhaps as many as three. Often the girl will own three separate mobile telephones, one for each lover so she doesn't get the name wrong when one of them calls. Then you have the very naive rice grower from Isaan who has heard about the money to be made in the big city, who spends a weekend hanging out at the bars on Sukhumvit, perhaps finds a man or two who hire her, only to discover she has not the slightest clue about foreign men, speaks not a word of English. She may be horrified and mystified by the very idea of oral sex and catches the next bus home to her farm in the north, never to

MONEY NUMBER ONE

visit the big city again. Then you have experts, very talented and attractive women who can literally wrap men around their fingers. Such girls often receive income from three or more foreign men, who live overseas and of course are unaware of each other, who are paying her to stay out of the bars until they arrive for their vacations. Of course, she continues to sell her body every night and is probably receiving a total income in excess of any middle-ranking professional, such as a lawyer or doctor.

"There is really no comparison between the destinies, mind-sets or lifestyles of these different women, but because they are all prostitutes we inadvertently find ourselves talking about them as if they were in the same plight, which they are not. The truth is that prostitution fulfils many functions. It is a substitute for social welfare, medical insurance, student loans, a profitable hobby as well as being the path to that wealth which many modern women expect from life. It also brings an enormous amount of foreign currency to our country, which means the government is never serious about suppressing it."

Most Bar Hostesses value cleanliness, take pride in their appearance and wear the neatest and most attractive clothing their finances will allow. This is in contrast to sweaty *farang* who, while roaming around town, appear to dress according to whatever yardage of scrap curtain material they can fit around their robust waistlines.

TIP
Here's a fashion tip: Wearing socks with sandals or open-toed shoes is to fashion what a turd sandwich is to cordon bleu.

Pattaya can be a great equalizer. After perhaps several divorces and raising children followed by years of rejections from any female remotely resembling human form, mature male visitors to Pattaya find the gap between the Hollywood sex symbol super stud and their own fault-ridden body has narrowed somewhat. Sure, it is all about money, but to an older man who's ego has been shattered by an oestrogen-dominated Western society transfixed on the body beautiful, what price is too high to pay for an end to his low self-esteem? It boils down to whether he prefers to live in a fool's paradise or a wise man's pergatory. He may not find true love but it is the closest he is going to get at this late stage of his life.

NEIL HUTCHISON

The Hostesses employed in Pattaya's adult entertainment industry appear not to care so much about physical appearance or age when it comes to their *farang* customers. It does not matter if a man is over seventy years of age, facially-challenged and has a beer gut that starts from his neck. He does not have to be a young movie star to attract the attention of one of Pattaya's Bar Hostesses. If the Elephant Man mated with The Hunchback of Notre Dame, the ugliest of their male offspring could find a girlfriend here, providing he had the financial means to support her in a manner to which she would like to become accustomed.

Many ladies truthfully admit they prefer to go with older men. It has been suggested this is because younger men are 'butterflies' (see Chapter 8) while an older man is more grateful for her attention, likely to have more money to pay for that attention and is generally not as demanding in the bedroom as his younger counterpart. I don't believe that for a minute.

MONEY NUMBER ONE

TIP

Expats speak volumes of the honesty, loyalty, sincerity and integrity shown to foreign men by Pattaya's Bar Hostesses. (For confirmation of this, simply ask any long-term foreign resident of Pattaya.) However, it won't hurt foreign men to be aware of her actual order of priorities. It goes as follows and the order never varies.

1. MONEY
2. GOLD
3. FOOD
4. SLEEPING
5. HER CHILD OR CHILDREN
6. GRANDPARENTS, MOTHER & FATHER
7. HER *REAL* THAI HUSBAND OR BOYFRIEND, SIBLINGS AND OTHER FAMILY MEMBERS
8. HER THAI FRIENDS
9. EVERY OTHER THAI PERSON IN THE WORLD, DOWN TO THE LOWLIEST BANGKOK BEGGAR
10. THE FAMILY BUFFALO (HEALTHY OR OTHERWISE)
11. PET DOG, CAT OR RAT
12. THE FLEAS ON PET DOG, CAT OR RAT
13. YOU

Whenever a choice has to be made between any of the above groups, they will always choose from the top down. Many a foreign male visitor has deluded himself into thinking that his importance to the lady is higher than it really is. When push comes to shove, he has been sadly mistaken.

That list has been discussed at length on Pattaya Internet forums and the general consensus is that it is correct. I could possibly slip 'Her mobile phone(s)' into position 4 which would move us down to Number 14, but I like the idea of us at Number 13 because it is such an unlucky number.

Surprisingly, I have shown the list to a number of Thai ladies and almost all of them agreed with it. They may laugh when they say it but, deep down, they know it is true. One girl working at one of my regular watering holes actually started calling me 'Number 13'!

In the interest of fairness, for this edition of *Money Number One* I have included a reprint of the list translated into Thai. Show it to your Thai wife, girlfriend or latest squeeze and ask for her opinion.

จัดลำดับความสำคัญสำหรับผู้หญิงไทย

1. เงิน
2. ทอง
3. อาหาร
4. นอนหลับ
5. ลูก ๆ ของเธอ
6. ปู่ย่าตายาย พ่อและแม่
7. สามีหรือแฟนคนไทยและพี่น้องของเธอ
8. เพื่อนคนไทยของเธอทั้งหมด
9. คนไทยทุกคนบนโลก
10. ความของครอบครัวเธอ (สบายหรือป่วย)
11. หมาสัตว์เลี้ยงหรือแมวหรือหนู
12. หมัดบนหมาสัตว์เลี้ยงหรือแมวหรือหนู
13. ฝรั่ง

MONEY NUMBER ONE
Life of a Pattaya Bar Hostess

"Before you criticize someone,
walk a mile in their shoes.
That way, if they get angry,
you are a mile away and you have their shoes!"

In Pattaya, the Bar Hostesses are mostly upcountry girls from poor rural communities and most are supporting or helping to support at least one other person. Those with a child or children of their own will often tell you, and it is difficult to accept they are being less than truthful here, the father was a Thai boyfriend who got her pregnant and then (in almost every case), shot through. Tragically, many of the girls have had their heart broken by Thai men who, although very charming, sweet and handsome, often lack a sense of responsibility toward their family duties. Her mother, friends or relatives in the province will be taking care of the child while the girl earns money to send home because the runaway boyfriend does not contribute financially.

> *In spite of what they may tell foreign customers, many of the Bar Hostesses still have a Thai boyfriend or husband. (NOT ALL, but the consensus among expats is around 80%.) Her activities are not kept secret from him either and, in many cases, not only does the boyfriend know about her profession, but more often than not, he encourages it. Whether he actively becomes her 'pimp' or not, the money she earns will go towards supporting him.*

With or without a boyfriend, husband or child, each month she will be sending money home to her parents. According to *Thailand Fever*, *"Thai children feel a life-long responsibility (debt of gratitude) to always help their parents (gat-dtan-yuu)."* Further, to those Westerners who assume her parents are pressuring her, *"as part of a scheme to make a profit using their beautiful child,"* the authors make the following comment: *"Little does he know that you help your parents because you want to, not because you have to!"*

That is generally true but, rightly or wrongly, Thailand's interaction with the West means more and more exceptions, particularly among the younger generation, are coming to light.

After working almost four years in a Go Go Bar, the lady left Pattaya because she had reached her goal of saving one million baht. She headed back to her village to build a house and set up a small business for herself. A year later, she was back working at the same Go Go Bar. Her friends and family had borrowed, stolen, drank, gambled or squandered her money on their own creature comforts until it was all gone. She was back to square one and, dare we suggest, less likely in the future to subsidize her family's lifestyle with any of her hard-earned savings.

Working conditions and salaries vary greatly from bar to bar and there is no enforceable statute declaring what the minimum should be. With plenty of jobs to choose from, the market dictates what is acceptable. A lady working at a Beer Bar for a full month may receive 3,000 *baht* for example. The cashier and *mamasan* will receive more than that, because they have less chance of getting lady drinks and no chance of being bar fined. The basic salary for a dancer in a Go Go Bar starts at around 6,000 *baht*. The service staff in a Go Go Bar will receive less.

This doesn't sound much but when her share of tips and her commission from lady drinks and bar fines are added, it would be rare for any employee to receive only her basic salary over the full month.

Working hours also vary greatly between bars. Beer Bars will operate either two twelve-hour shifts or three eight-hour shifts, with the lucrative night shift beginning at say 5:00pm and finishing at 1:00am. The day shift may only have a skeleton staff of a handful of ladies. Go Go Bars which operate in the afternoon have two shifts; the first from 1:00pm to 7:00pm and the second from 7:00pm until whatever closing time is currently in force. Some ladies can work both shifts if they wish, or pick which one they prefer. Some work the afternoon shift then head to Walking Street for another shift at a Go Go Bar where the late night pickings are better.

TIP
Always a good idea to find out beforehand whether a lady has two jobs. Say you fall in love with a Go Go dancer at 4:00pm and decide you would like her companionship for the entire evening. Her bar fine of 500 baht could become 1,000 baht if she has to start work again at 7:00pm. Either that or she will have to be back at the bar in time for her second shift. One

MONEY NUMBER ONE

option is to wait until 7:00pm before making your move, knowing that if someone else bar fines her in the meantime, you have simply missed your turn.

When a customer buys a lady drink (charging from 90 to 150 *baht*), she receives a commission of between 30 and 50 *baht*. Other tips received from customers are divided among all the staff at the end of each shift. This is why some bars ask customers to '*check bin*' at the shift changeover. You don't have to leave, merely start a new *bin*.

If a lady is absent because she has been bar fined, the money is put aside for her to collect later. The amount paid to each lady in this way provides for her day-to-day living expenses.

TIP
Once you pay your bill, any money left on the little silver tray is divided among all the staff. If a particular Hostess was very good to you and you want to show your appreciation only to her, when you 'check bin' place the tip directly into her hand. She can keep any money that you give to her directly.

If she elects to accompany a customer for a night at the cinema, he will pay the bar fine which, in Beer Bars, starts from 250 *baht*. (Although with rising inflation you would be hard pressed to find any bar still charging that little.) The lady will receive upwards of 50 *baht* from that. Whatever money she receives from the customer after that is hers. If for some reason she does not want to work one night, she must pay her own bar fine. If she goes with the same *farang* for more than one night, he must pay the bar fine for each night he is with her.

Most Bar Hostesses live in apartments which they share with as many as four other people. The monthly rent will be from 2,500 to 4,500 *baht*, plus another 500 *baht* for electricity and water. Therefore, each lady sharing the room is up for around 1,500 *baht* per month for her accommodation. Her basic salary, usually paid on the first of the month, covers these fixed expenses plus the money she sends to her family. Often depleted within two or three days, she is left to live on tips, lady drink commissions and bar fines for the rest of the month.

She will spend up to 100 *baht* per day on food (Thai food is not expensive if you know where to go and many bar owners provide free meals for their staff). In an average month, she could cover this amount.

In low season, maybe not. In high season, it would not be much of a problem. However, the only way for her to save money or increase her own quality of life by way of new clothes, treats and holidays is to find a generous customer.

Of course, a few local ladies make an absolute fortune by accumulating a stable of generous foreign boyfriends. Some of these are true 'professionals' to the extent they could be described as being totally greedy, selfish and cunning to the point of evil. They want it all and don't care how they get it or who they hurt in the process. But the vast majority of Pattaya Bar Hostesses are not like that. Most of them simply make a sustainable living. At least it is more money than they could earn selling chewing gum back home in the province.

When her outgoings become too high, the girl can sometimes borrow money from the bar or her friends who have had better luck. Watching 'pay day' in a bar is an absolute hoot. Money changes hands in an organised frenzy as debts are repaid and recouped.

If all else fails, then there are characters who visit the bars and discreetly loan the girls money. This works on the Chinese '6 for 5' system. I loan you 5 and at the end of the month you pay back 6. The guy will lend the girl 1,000 *baht* and every day for the next 30 days she will pay back 40 *baht*. If she misses one payment, the next night she has to pay back 80 *baht*. At the end of 30 days, any outstanding balance becomes the '5' and she then owes 120% of that amount. The complexities of compound interest have not sunk into the average bar worker. If your stomach is empty and you have no money, it does not seem to be important.

Freelancers

Some ladies appearing to work as Bar Hostesses are not on salary but operate as 'freelancers' who come and go as they please. Often they are part-timers, holding down a day job while working at night for tips, drinks and the prospect of meeting a generous *farang*. These ladies usually have a few favourite places to hang out so if there are no customers in one they move on to another. Many freelancers are migratory - they will work in Pattaya during the high season then Bangkok or Chiang Mai for the rest of the year because there is less of a low season in those places.

Other freelance operators do not linger at any bar but hang around places frequented by *farang* in the hope of attracting the attention and affection of one. They can be found in discos, nightclubs and coffee shops

MONEY NUMBER ONE

or walking or sitting along Beach Road, especially towards the South Pattaya end. In Bangkok, many can be found in the evenings sitting at the plentiful Thai food stalls along Sukhumvit Road in the Nana area (*Soi* 4), in the Bier Garden (*Soi* 7/1) or at *Thermae's* Coffee Shop (*Soi* 13). NEVER automatically assume any attractive lady you see in these areas is a freelancer. She may simply be out for a stroll or a meal and it is very insulting to a Thai female to be mistakenly thought of in that way. You will make no friends.

Many Beer Bar owners will allow freelancers to use their bar, especially if they are attractive and he is short of salaried staff. The condition is that a bar fine is payable should a customer wish to take her out of the bar and 'lady drink' prices are charged for her drinks. The customer will probably only have to pay the bar fine for the first night. After that, private arrangements can be made and it will not be required. The benefit of finding a freelancer outside a bar is that you don't have to pay any bar fine or pay for lady drinks. Unfortunately, there are also things to be wary of:

1. Never go to her room for your intimate encounter. A few men have done this only to discover, too late, they were not alone in the room. Her boyfriend or accomplice was hiding and waiting to accost or rifle through the wallet of the unsuspecting customer while he was otherwise occupied. Some men have accepted a drink offered by their new friend only to wake up the next morning with a severe headache, no money, no clothes and no sign of the girl. These guys were lucky – at least they woke up.

2. Some freelance girls are not really 'girls' at all, but what the Thais call *katoeys* or 'lady-boys'. It is dark, they are beautiful, you are drunk and by the time you get back to your room and find out the truth, it is too late. Should you be inclined to discontinue the relationship, it will often cost you money just to get rid of her/him.

3. If anything unfortunate does happen to you during the course of the relationship, you have no recourse. What are you going to tell the police? "Yes officer, her name was *Lek*, she was short, had black hair, brown eyes, was wearing blue jeans and I met her on Beach Road." The police will laugh you out of their office faster than you can say, "I'm a stupid *farang*".

Another twist was reported in the Pattaya Mail of February 2004. At around 2:00am police were called to an apartment building after staff reported an incident. Officers arrived at the room to find a Thai woman crying with a foreigner standing nearby. The woman pointed to him saying that he had raped her. Both were taken to the Police Station for questioning.

The man told police he was walking along Beach Road when he met the woman. They sat, chatted and agreed on a price for services before going back to his room. Once their activities were finished, he paid the agreed rate but the woman demanded more. He refused and tried to remove her from the room, at which time she began screaming.

Her side of the story was that she was sitting on the beachfront when the man approached her. They chatted and he asked her to go back to his room for a massage for 300 baht. She alleged, during the massage, the foreigner became amorous and forced her to have sex. Afterwards he released her and tried to kick her out of the room, at which time she called for help.

Police recorded the statements and the woman was sent to a hospital for medical examination. She returned to the station to proceed with her claims. The man asked police if he could settle the matter with the woman and they came to an agreement of 4,500 baht. Officers then released the pair on their own accord.

That story is not unique and other men have reported taking a freelancer back to their room where she either flatly refused to be intimate or made up some excuse. She then demanded money to leave, threatening to call the hotel manager (and subsequently the police) if he did not comply.

4. A few freelancers may not have yet reached 18 years of age. Whenever in doubt, politely ask to see her ID card and do not accept any excuses for her not showing it to you. If you take her back to your hotel, show her ID card to the receptionist and ask them to confirm the lady is over 18. The Buddhist calendar is 543 years older than the Gregorian one, which means for a lady to be 18 in the year 2013, her ID card must show she was born in or before the year 2538. The latest Thai National ID Cards have the date of birth in English as well. Always be careful!

MONEY NUMBER ONE

One scam operated along Beach Road involved a 15-year-old girl (she was well-developed and looked to be in her twenties) who was coerced by her mother to go with men. After the encounter, the customer would be confronted by the 'outraged' mother who would reveal the true age of the girl. "If you don't want me to call the police, it will cost you 50,000 baht."

In spite of these added precautions, many *farang* have reported meeting some very nice ladies working part-time as freelancers away from the bar scene. Genuine and honest people can be found in every walk of life so, in the final analysis, it is up to you.

Exotic Language of the Bars

The Thai word '*farang*' is not a derogatory term so don't get upset when you are constantly referred to as a *farang*. Literally, it means foreigner, Westerner, or European. One opinion is it is derived from the Thai pronunciation of the word 'francais'. The early Thai would have had significant interaction with the French who had colonized Indochina, what is now Cambodia and Vietnam. The Thai translated the word 'francais' as *fa-rang-sayt*. This was later shortened and used to refer to all Europeans, not just the French.

Another opinion is it comes from the Portuguese. The Portuguese language became the language of trade through most of Asia during much of the 16th century. To Asians, the Portuguese were known as *feringhi*.

Whatever its correct derivation, in modern Pattaya the 'r' is sounded as an 'l' and the word is pronounced 'fa-lung', to rhyme with 'dung', 'hung', 'lung', 'sung' and 'tongue'.

You probably know that Thai is a tonal language. Words are spoken with a high tone, mid tone, low tone, falling tone or rising tone. What you probably don't know is that, in an attempt to express their true opinion of you as a foreigner, the Bar Hostesses add the English adjective 'Stupid' before the noun *farang*. (This is contrary to Thai grammar which states you should always place the adjective after the noun.) They give the word 'Stupid' a low tone - a very low tone. So low, in fact, that most of the time it is inaudible. Never forget, whether you hear it or not, your title is always 'Stupid *farang*'.

One common English expression used by the Hostesses of the bars is "Up to you". Along with, "Hello sexy man", "Sit down please" and "What you like some drink?" it must be one of the first English phrases they learn. Although implying that you are in the position of power, it can wear you down when you are continually given "Up to you" as the response to questions to which you genuinely would like an opinion or suggestion.

"Where would you like to go?"   "Up to you."
"How much money do you want?"   "Up to you."
"What is your name?"   "Up to you."
"Do you really love me?"   "Up to you."

All jokes aside, the basic premise is absolutely true. It *is* up to you. Americans put it another way – "It's your dime".

TIP
Never forget that you are the one who is paying to be entertained, not the other way round. It does not make a lot of sense to be paying a small fortune to be somewhere you do not want to be, doing something you do not want to do, with someone you do not want to be with. Stupid farang!

Hidden beneath the language of the Bar Hostesses, there are three given truths to be aware of:

1. Any girl working in a bar, and all those who previously worked in a bar, only ever work or worked as 'cashier'.

   Q: How do you confuse bar girls?
   A: Write a letter to a bar addressed simply to the 'Cashier'.
   Q: How do you create havoc at a bar?
   A: Address the envelope as above but make the letter as vague and brief as possible. Mention that you want her to e-mail you her bank account details so you can send her $1,000 to help out with her 'problem'. If that doesn't start World War III in the bar, nothing will!

2. The Bar Hostesses are there to provide companionship only and none of them ever have sex with a customer. If she stays the night with him, it is only to sleep.
3. Every girl working in the bar has a 'problem' at home that can be easily solved by a substantial injection of foreign money.

MONEY NUMBER ONE

Ok, so they may not strictly be 'truths', but this is Pattaya and truth is in short supply. For example, you return to a bar to see a lady you had been with on a previous occasion. She is not there and you are told, "She go room. Have stomach ache," or maybe, "She have to go home. Mama have problem." This, of course, is total bullshit. She has probably gone with another *farang*. You will never get the truth out of any of her friends at the bar, so don't bother pressing the subject. When (or if) you see her again, she will stick to the same story. Remember the one-legged chicken story?

He had only been in Pattaya four days and had been with the same girl since the night he arrived. Everything was great, she was great, the world was great, etc. Sadly, he was going to be on his own for a couple of days because Lek had to go home for Christmas. His expat friend felt obliged to tell him that there was a possibility (read: 100% certainty) that she may not be telling the truth. Thais do not usually celebrate Christmas in the villages so it was possible that she had another farang, a regular boyfriend perhaps, coming to Pattaya over that period. He responded confidently, "No. I'm sure she's sincere."

Two nights later his friend ran into him while he was walking around by himself and invited him for a drink at a bar in Naklua. Guess who they found sitting lovingly with another farang at one of the bars nearby? The guy meekly said, "Hello," to her as they passed.

"I did warn you," his friend told him.

He replied, "I know, but she seemed so genuine!"

They all do.

Money Number One! It would be rare for any Bar Hostess to give up the money she could get from you for any other reason than the possibility she will get more money from someone else. If she can keep you 'on hold' for a while, all the better.

The Bar Hostess went with one farang boyfriend to the airport and tearfully waved him goodbye from the departure area before heading straight to the arrivals section to meet her other boyfriend due to arrive an hour later. Was it luck or unbelievable organizational skills?

Bar Hostess v *Farang*

Imagine, if you will, that you are about to go to war, a war in which you believe you have the advantage. You have all the fire-power, the education, the experience and such a variety of choices that you should win hands down. Further imagine that you go into this war cocksure and confident of victory only to find that the enemy has one or two tricks up their sleeve you were unaware of. The enemy is a lot smarter than you gave them credit for and they have at their disposal an arsenal of weapons that you could not have imagined. What you thought would be an easy victory turns out to be a war of attrition and you find yourself out of ammunition and with your back to the wall.

No, I am not talking about Vietnam, Iraq or Afghanistan, but about the only war which really matters – the battle of the sexes. In particular, the battle of wits fought every day in hundreds of bars throughout Thailand – Bar Hostess v *Farang*.

Each day, foreign men arrive in this wonderful country with pockets full of money and heads full of the wrong attitude. Those who come believing that with their spending power and the availability of women, they have such an advantage they cannot lose, go home scratching their heads wondering where it all went. Sure they had a great time but, in a place where almost everything is cheaper than in their own country, "How did I end up spending so much money?"

The answer is simple. They underestimated the intelligence and resolve of the enemy, specifically, the Bar Hostesses. It is all one big mind game which the ladies are so good at that most *farang* don't even know they have been playing until it is all over.

Modern warfare, Pattaya style, consists of four distinct strategies - The Bait, The Intelligence Gathering, The Reassurance and The Flattery. There are no Rules of Engagement, no Geneva Conventions and no prisoners. She has already identified her opponent's weaknesses; his ignorance, his ego and his overconfidence. After that, it is impossible to describe all her military manoeuvres but, in each encounter, she uses her most lethal weapons; a youthful beauty, a cheeky smile and a sweet mouth.

The fun begins the moment he steps outside the sanctuary of his hotel room.

MONEY NUMBER ONE

First Wave – The Bait

Pattaya Bar Hostesses soon realize that foreign men find them very attractive. Thai males are drawn to girls with lighter skin tones, but even the ladies with darker skin learn that foreign men still find them attractive. All she has to do is keep clean, dress to the best her finances will allow and perhaps dab on a bit of war paint from time to time. The problem is, because men find so many of them attractive, the competition within the bars is fierce. The smarter girls quickly pick up a few key words of English and learn to take full advantage of their beautiful smile and seductive eyes.

Once she casts her eye upon an unsuspecting target, her sweet mouth fires the first Exocet of the battle and directs it towards every man's Achilles' Heel, his ego. It comes in the form of the classic, "Hello sexy man." There are doubts whether many of them know the full ramifications of the statement, but what they do know is that it is a winner; a tried and true moneyspinner. The advantage of her not understanding the words means she can keep a straight face while saying them.

It comes as a pleasant shock to the male psyche to be continually told by beautiful young women that he is a sexy man. The danger for the *farang* is that, if he is told the same lie often enough, he may start to believe it. Maybe all the females back home are wrong. Maybe the mirrors are distorted and his doctors are jealous of the way he has kept in shape over the years. "Hey, maybe I am a sexy man – a three hundred pound, old, bald, badly-dressed, genuinely sexy man!"

TIP

The antidote is soberingly simple. Before you go out each night, shower and stand naked in front of a full-length mirror, repeating aloud: "The women back home, the mirrors and the doctors who told me they have never seen a body like mine outside a jar of formaldehyde are correct. I am ugly. The only reason I am even remotely appealing is that I portray an image of wealth. I am disgusting but look like I have money." This medicine, although painful to swallow, is usually good for twenty-four hours.

NEIL HUTCHISON

Second Wave – Intelligence Gathering

Knowledge is power so, to gain an advantage, she needs to collect as much information about her adversary as possible. After initial pleasantries are exchanged between the *farang* and the Hostess designated to be his inquisitor, he will be asked his name, what country he comes from and how long he is staying. This sounds like simply polite conversation, but there is a deeper purpose to these questions.

> *The newly-arrived visitor inquired, "Why is she asking me all these questions?" His friend replied that she was merely gathering intelligence. "Good. It looks like she could certainly use some." Alas, the visitor was an empty MasterCard just waiting to happen.*

His name is required for identification and along with his nationality, forms a unique bar code for future reference. He is John-from-England or Peter-from-America or Hans-from-Germany and each Hostess will then know who the other girls are talking about. His nationality is also required for currency conversion. Should he be short of *baht* and pay the girl in dollars, pounds or euros, she has to know the exchange rate to calculate what she is getting and more importantly, if she is being short-changed.

"How long are you staying?" comes as part of a trilogy of related questions; "This your first time Thailand?" and "How long have you been here?" being the other two. General interest questions? Yes. Innocuous? No.

If he is on his first visit to Thailand he is neither street-wise nor bar-wise and he is easy game for a clever Bar Hostess. (One Go Go dancer actually confessed she used this information to work out how much she was going to charge him. A new kid on the block is less likely to know what the local going rate is so she would ask for more.) If he has been here for only one or two days, then he still has plenty of money to spend and if he is staying for another week or so, she has plenty of time to get it. He is a 'Class A Golden Goose', the most sought after prey for any Bar Hostess and she will fight tooth and nail to attract and hold his attention.

At the bottom of the scale is the 'Class Z Waste Of Time'. He is the bar-wise *farang* who has either been to Thailand many times, has stayed here for a long time or is more or less a resident. (Note: 'wise' is a relative term and in this context merely means 'wiser than totally stupid'.) This

MONEY NUMBER ONE

guy, if he tells them the truth, is given short shrift by the Hostesses and is looked upon with disdain for taking up a valuable seat which could otherwise be occupied by a Class A, B or C *farang*.

Fortunately, these guys rarely tell the truth and so the Hostesses have to look for more subtle signs before they can relegate him to the Bar Twilight Zone with the beggars, lepers, *farang* with no money and other undesirables.

Half way down the ladder is the 'Class M *Hah-sip Hah-sip*' [50-50] *farang*. You can figure out for yourself what half way between Class A and Class Z is, but a Bar Hostess will have to ask further questions before determining if he is a bankable commodity. Since it is not his first time in Thailand, the first question is whether or not he already has a Thai wife or girlfriend. The second is whether he can speak Thai. An answer in the affirmative to either of these questions and he immediately slides to Class Z. A negative response means that she must use more complex methods of assessment.

Not all the intelligence gathering is verbal. Bar Hostesses are skilled at reading body language and picking up subtle signs as to a person's character. Within thirty minutes, the more experienced ones will know approximately how much money he has, what pocket he keeps it in, whether he is a Cheap Charlie or has a 'good heart' and how much of the folding stuff he would be likely to part with for her company for an evening.

Once the interrogation and evaluation is complete, he can be mentally tagged and pigeonholed. Now it is up to each individual Bar Hostess to decide how much effort she will put in to earn his favour. This is where it gets interesting because she has calculated her potential rewards and knows how much ammunition she is willing to expend.

Depending largely on the number of alternative options available in the form of other customers, some ladies will decide he is not worth the effort and politely retreat. If she does choose to continue the fight, she will plan the next wave of her attack. This comes in the form of making reassuring comments about herself.

Third Wave – The Reassurance

The Bar Hostesses have this down to a fine art. In amongst the bamboo English there are the standard lines. It makes you wonder where they get this stuff because they are always the same lines, word for word, and each comes in almost identical order. Is there a book for Bar Hostesses listing all the lines that can be spun to gullible *farang*? Maybe there is a secret school in some out of the way *soi* where it is taught. In any event, once they have his undivided attention, the bullshit will run thicker than molasses.

The most popular is the, "I no like work bar," line which may, in fact, be true. This is sometimes coupled with, "I only work bar one month." The fact that she may have been working in bars for five years and only worked at that particular bar for one month is inconsequential. The idea is to give you the impression that she is not really like the rest of them. She is not really a bar girl. She may reinforce the point by actually saying, "I not same lady bar."

In the past, the girls who actually admitted they had worked in other bars would add the line "But I only work cashier," to this barrage of bullshit. Nowadays it seems they have finally realized that *farang* are not quite as stupid as they look. Even the most myopic foreigner has correctly concluded that there are not ten thousand cashiers employed in the bars of Pattaya.

Many Bar Hostesses are aware that foreign men are deeply jealous of Thai men, whether it is warranted or not. She must now attempt to distance herself from Thai men and ingratiate herself with the foreigner. "I no like Thai man," is the wording and it will come out after any general question regarding her past Thai boyfriends. Every Bar Hostess will tell you the same thing even though many still have a Thai boyfriend, lover or husband. Thailand did not become the most ethnically pure nation in South East Asia because the female population do not like the male population.

By the end of this wave of her attack, if the *farang* is still showing interest, she has assured him of her situation. She really is a nice girl who has been obliged to do something that she does not want to do through tragic but temporary economic necessity.

In short, "She is different."

MONEY NUMBER ONE

"I never go with *farang* before. I only work cashier."

NEIL HUTCHISON

The Final Assault – The Flattery

Convincing him that she really is a wonderful person is not quite enough. She now has to convince him that she does really, truly, cross-my-heart-and-hope-to-die like him. The nature of a male is such that his ego or conscience will make it difficult for him to dislike any female who professes that she likes him and is attracted to him. Women throughout the world know this and they all use it to their advantage.

> *"The reason that adulation is not displeasing is that, though untrue, it shows one to be of consequence enough, in one way or other, to induce people to lie."*
> Lord Byron (1788–1824), English poet.

If he is young, say under thirty, she will begin with, "I like young man. No like old man." If he is older than dirt he will hear, "I like old man. No like young man." If he initially told her he was from America, "I like man America. No like man England." If he is from the UK, "I like man England. No like man America." If he is fat, she will respond with, "I like man *poong ploo-ee*." She may go even further and point to her own 45kg frame and declare that she too is *poong ploo-ee* [fat].

If his complexion is snow white, she will tell him how much she likes white skin. She may point out how dark her own skin is and express her desire to be white like him. If he is as bald as a billiard ball, covered in tattoos, has earrings, nose-rings, missing teeth and wears horned-rimmed glasses, she will remark how much she likes each of these features and sum up by insisting that the overall combination makes him one hell of an attractive man.

With that, the battle has been waged and it is simply a matter of waiting for the result. There is no necessity to contemplate what makes the *farang* the victor because such an outcome is beyond the realms of possibility. The best he can hope for is to walk away calling it a draw.

The lady, on the other hand, claims outright victory immediately the *farang* raises the white flag by asking that immortal question: "How much is your bar fine?"

Gotcha!

MONEY NUMBER ONE

"Hello sexy man!"

Bar Speak

In 2009, a friend showed me a pocket-sized, 138-page booklet entitled, *Get Rich Quick English for Bar Girls* (2nd. Edition), created by the SHELL Program Co., Ltd. This was like finding the 'missing link'. As mentioned earlier, I knew such a book had to exist but I just hadn't found it yet.

It is uncertain how long the book has been in circulation but, considering it was the "2nd. Edition", it must have been out for a few years at least. One thing for sure, it has been kept very secret.

The book is a compilation of every possible English phrase a modern, successful Bar Hostess should know, complete with the Thai translation and a phonetic English transliteration.

For instance (and I am not making this up), early in the book is, "I love you, not your money." Later there are some very intimate phrases. "You've got a big one," is a classic while "What turns you on?" should be mandatory. There are many others which even made me blush.

The last chapter is headed "Asking Money from Client," and includes such gems as:

"Do you like spending time with me?"
"Would you like to see me again?"
"May I have some money for last night?"
"I enjoyed last night very much and you were very good."
"If you pay me well, I'll do it better next time."
"If you pay me well, we'll have more fun next time."
"I enjoyed our time together. Do you mind if I ask you for some money?"

So, to the question; "Is there a book for Bar Hostesses listing all the lines that can be spun to gullible *farang*?"; the answer is a resounding "YES".

Putting aside the urge to have the publisher charged with treason, all is not lost and two can play at that game. The counter move requires foreigners to understand the true meaning behind the Bar Hostess' sweet words.

What follows are the most common lines told to *farang* males by Bar Hostesses. The list, compiled over the last decade, is by no means complete.

MONEY NUMBER ONE

If she says ...	She REALLY means ...
Hello sexy man.	Hello stupid *farang*.
Hello. Sit down please.	Hello. Come in sucker.
You very handsome/sexy man.	You look like you have a lot of money.
Where you come from?	What currency do I need to check the exchange rate?
Your first time Thailand?	Just how gullible are you?
I no have farang. Farang not like me.	I have many *farang*. Going for your sympathy vote works every time.
How long you stay Thailand?	How long have I got to bleed you dry?
Which hotel you stay?	Where will I be sleeping tonight?
You want play game?	Buy me a drink, dickhead.
You have Thai lady?	Do I have to share your money with anyone else?
I no like Thai man. <u>or</u> *I no have Thai boyfriend.*	I have a Thai boyfriend and I use all the money I make to support him.
I love you.	I love your money.
You have good heart.	You have a big wallet.
You good man for me.	You are spending a lot of money. You are good for my bank account.
I miss you.	I miss your money.
I no want money.	I want your money.
I no want money. Only want you.	I want all your money.
I go with you for free.	This will cost you double.
I no butterfly.	I only sleep with my boyfriend and any *farang* who pays my bar fine.
I no like work bar.	Working bar is easier than working in a factory.

NEIL HUTCHISON

If she says …	**She REALLY means …**
I only work cashier.	I am a liar.
I go with him before, but no boomsing.	I truly am a liar.
I not lie. I no like goh-hok.	I am a BIG liar.
She same same my sister.	We met for the first time last night.
I wait for you till you come back Thailand.	I will wait until you are securely on the plane home.
My friend me.	My boyfriend.
My friend you.	Your friend.
Money me.	My money.
Money you.	My money.
We go to XYZ Bar tonight?	I owe drinks to some friends at XYZ Bar. You can pay.
I need 4,000 baht to give my Mama for…	My boyfriend needs new tyres for his motorcycle.
You give me 10,000 baht now and I stay with you for two weeks.	You give me 10,000 baht now and you will never see me or the money again.
I never cheat.	When you look, I never cheat. When you don't look, I cheat.
You can not come my apartment. It not clean.	You cannot come to my apartment because my boyfriend is there sleeping off a hangover.
Money Number One!	Money Number One!

7
General Observations

Experience is the best teacher and this is particularly true of Thailand. In fact, here experience is the only teacher and all the advice under the sun is meaningless without it. For what it is worth, the following notes may help you save money while traversing the cultural minefield that is Thailand and gaining that much-needed experience.

1   Thai Bar Hostesses like to have fun. *Sanook sanook.* They like to laugh, play games, joke, kid around and be happy and tend to avoid the company of people who are sad or miserable. If you are seen to be a 'fun' person they will be attracted to you and want to be with you. If you treat them well and they enjoy being with you, they will repay you by taking genuine care of you while not attempting to extract extra money from you at every opportunity. Treat every lady you are with, whether it be for one hour or one year, as if she were your one and only girlfriend. Show her kindness and respect and you will be repaid in kind. This is not to say that you should let your guard down, but you will have a lot more fun.

NEIL HUTCHISON

2. Once you have decided that you enjoy the company of a particular Hostess, don't just assume she is yours for the taking. Ask her if she wants to go with you. If she agrees, pay the bar fine and *check bin* immediately. Do not stay at that bar and do not come back later with her. Even if the night is still young and you do not wish to return to your room, leave that bar and go to another one not too close by. The reasons for this are twofold:

   a) While you have been buying drinks for the woman of your dreams, before you paid the bar fine, she receives a commission on each 'lady drink'. Her drinks are more expensive than if you had brought the same drink for yourself. After you pay the bar fine, theoretically her working day at that bar is over and she becomes a customer, not an employee. Therefore her drinks should be the normal price. This rarely happens and many ladies will want to keep you at the bar, still filling your *bin* and collecting their commission on each drink. By going to another bar you can avoid this added expense.

   b) As mentioned earlier, the Bar Hostesses form a type of sorority. Your angel may share a room with some of the others. As a 'sisterhood', they help each other out in times of need. Your lady may even owe a few favours. Once it is seen that she has snared herself a *farang*, these favours may be politely called in (you won't understand because the conversation will be in Thai). All you will hear from your delightful companion is, "You buy my friend a drink? She no have money." You will be surprised at how many 'friends' she has that suddenly pop over to say hello. Getting caught many times with this trick can be expensive.

   TIP
   Instead of buying lady drinks all night, buy the first one for the apple of your eye and quietly tell her that if she stays with you and does not ask you for another drink, you will give her 100 baht tip when you check bin. She will usually agree although some bars, especially Go Go Bars, have a policy whereby each lady must get a minimum number of 'lady drinks' each month or her salary is cut. If it is near the end of the month and she is short of her quota, she may decline your offer.

MONEY NUMBER ONE

3 Once you have enjoyed the companionship of a Hostess from a particular bar and for whatever reason have decided that you do not wish to go with her again, it is considered bad manners to return to that bar and select another girl. Your first girl will lose face in front of her friends and your second choice will be put off by the fact that you did not pick her the first time. Choose carefully the first time. One way out is, when on your next trip to the bar, your original choice has already gone with or is busy entertaining another *farang*. It is then OK to select another girl and nobody loses face. Of course, you now have a problem if you go back a third time to find both girls available. How to get out of it is one of life's unsolved mysteries. The only advice is to make sure neither girl loses face in front of her friends.

4 When you are with your girl, do not go to a bar, shop or restaurant of her choosing. If she says "We go here," then go somewhere else. More often than not, she will have friends or relatives at that particular establishment and she will be eager to repay outstanding favours or debts with your money. Either that or she may be getting a commission from your purchases. This is not always the case and some girls do genuinely look after you when it comes to saving you from being overcharged.

At a Beer Bar one evening, my friend decided to buy his new lady a nice dress from a passing street vendor. The vendor asked for 160 baht, but before my friend reached for his wallet the lady bargained with the vendor who finally agreed to a price of 140 baht. Even though it was only 20 baht, that lady did more to restore my faith in Thai womanhood than she could ever imagine.

5 Do not get sucked into buying flowers for the new love of your life. Buying flowers for your *farang* wife or girlfriend is a wonderful romantic gesture and she may go weak at the knees with such a thoughtful loving gift. Pattaya Bar Hostesses could not care less about receiving flowers and one even lamented, in all seriousness, "I cannot eat flowers." Receiving a bunch of flowers from you evokes the same feeling that you get when someone buys you a pair of socks or a handkerchief for your birthday. Don't waste your money. Buying

her one of those cuddly stuffed toys is almost as bad. Many Bar Hostesses' apartments are filled with a veritable zoo of stuffed animals of all shapes and sizes and not one of the girls can remember who gave her what.

6   If you wish to give the object of your devotion a gift, the only things that Thai Bar Hostesses truly appreciate are money (Number One) and gold. Pure 24k gold or Thai gold (22k) only - none of that 18k or gold-plated rubbish. The gold they want comes in the form of a necklace, chain, bracelet or ring. It is sold by weight and, in Thailand, the unit of weight is called a '*baht*'. This is not to be confused with the Thai currency which is also called a '*baht*'. One '*baht*' of gold weighs around 15.16 grams and the price depends on the current world gold price. For example, in January 2013 one '*baht*' of gold will cost you upwards of 24,500 *baht* in Thai currency. As well as being an adornment, her gold is a 'safety net' and if ever she is desperate for money she can always sell or pawn it.

He remembers buying his first gold chain. His girlfriend picked it out after much deliberation and was truly delighted as they headed for the front door with her new adornment hanging triumphantly from her gorgeous neck. He should have twigged when the gold shop owner farewelled him with "See you again soon," as they hurried outside. Over the next twelve months, he ended up buying that same gold chain three times.

Gold is also a status symbol. By flaunting her gold jewellery, the other girls will know that she has a kind and generous *farang* taking care of her. *Jai dee!* She has moved up a rung on the Bar Hostesses' social ladder.

He bought his girlfriend a beautiful dress ring for her birthday. That evening when they went out to dinner, he was surprised to see that she was not wearing the ring. She made some feeble excuse but later she questioned him regarding the 'silver' appearance of the metal in the ring. The penny dropped. She did not wear the ring because she thought it was silver. He explained to her that it was not silver but in fact 'white gold' or a platinum/gold alloy which was much more expensive than

MONEY NUMBER ONE

"When I say you buy me five baht gold,
I not mean you give me five baht!"

gold. (In truth, it was probably stainless steel or tin, going by what he paid for it in a Hong Kong street market). Her greedy little eyes lit up and she reached into her purse, pulled out the ring and slipped it on her delicate finger. His girl and he have since split up under not the best of circumstances. One of the few little pleasures he has in life is picturing the little darling trying to convince a Thai gold shop owner that her ring was very expensive platinum when she went to sell it five minutes after they parted company.

7   The only other gift that a Thai Bar Hostess may appreciate is clothes, especially shoes. It appears there is a little Imelda Marcos in all women. Don't initiate the purchase yourself. Let her see something she really likes and then, if you are feeling exceptionally loving or benevolent, offer to buy it for her. Be careful. You will have then set a precedent and thereafter, every time she sees something she likes, your hand (or hers) will be reaching for your wallet. Let it be known that your gift is a one-off for something special and not a daily event. If you have limited finances, avoid buying from the big tourist-oriented shopping centres. Inexpensive clothing can be purchased from the markets. In Pattaya, two markets worth a visit are the *Soi* Buakow day market (corner South Pattaya Road) on Tuesdays and Fridays and the Thepprasit Road night market (corner Sukhumvit Road) on Friday, Saturday and Sunday nights.

8   One last comment on gift giving. When you give a Thai person a present that is giftwrapped, do not expect them to open it then and there in front of you. Thai custom is to put the present aside and open it later when they are alone. This way, a Bar Hostess can avoid an obvious display of disappointment if the gift turns out to be something she less than appreciates.

9   When taking your wonderful Thai companion out for a meal it is both easy and convenient to allow her to order for the both of you. This presents a fantastic opportunity for your new friend to show off the bounty of delicious food available in this remarkable country. She may be keen to order a maximum number of dishes to demonstrate the variety of delicious tastes and flavours, so you may discover the dining table covered with plate after bowl after dish of

MONEY NUMBER ONE

"See you again soon!"

delicious food for your epicurean inspection. She will sample each dish to ensure they reach the usual first-rate culinary standard of Thailand. When she sits back and says, *"im"*, maybe even with a gentle pat to her taut stomach, it means she is full.

TIP
For those who are not big eaters, before your Thai companion orders, you could explain politely that you are not very hungry, even if you are starving. She will still be excited about showing off her fabulous country's superior cuisine, but may decide to do it over a period of time rather than at the one sitting. After she has carefully tasted a mouthful from each dish and declared she is "im", you can then eat the remaining food to show your appreciation.

10 Being a man of the world, you probably realize by now that women are strange animals indeed. Women can be very moody and temperamental at times. The Bar Hostesses of Pattaya are no exception and can change moods in an instant, without provocation and definitely without warning. A full 180° turnaround. Hell hath no fury like a pissed-off Thai Bar Hostess.
Initially, she becomes very vocal. (The authors of those books on Thai culture stating that Thais never raise their voices are living in fantasyland.) Thankfully you will not understand a word as she rattles off abuse in machinegun Thai. (Many revert to speaking their native Isaan dialect or even Lao because, so I am told, there are a lot more swear words to choose from.) Next, she becomes very physical and very destructive. Once you have picked a Bar Hostess's mood changing for the worse, remove from her presence, or remove her from the presence of, all sharp or heavy objects. Follow this by distancing her from anything that belongs to you. The objects on which she vents her anger will belong to you rather than her. The girls become irrational, not stupid.

One guy made the mistake of walking out of his apartment once he realized that his girlfriend was in a severely agitated state. He returned later to find that his normally docile mate had used his golf clubs to obliterate his TV and stereo system. Then, for good measure, she had destroyed his golf clubs.

MONEY NUMBER ONE

She may be keen to order a maximum number
of dishes to demonstrate a variety
of delicious tastes to your unworthy palate.

Once you have ensured the safety of your personal property, distance yourself from her and give her time to cool down. There is nothing to be gained by staying around and arguing with her. (Refer Chapter 4, Lesson Four – Reasoning and Logic) With nobody to rant and rave at, her mood may change back to normal just as quickly as it went off the rails. The fun part is that you will probably never know what you did wrong in the first place.

11 If you are 100% heterosexual there is an extra precaution you should take. Thailand has its share of *katoeys* ('ladyboys', transsexuals or transvestites) and some of them are incredibly beautiful. Follow this rule: If you suspect in the slightest that the newfound object of your lust could possibly be a male, then he/she/it is. If you are still unsure, quietly ask one of the other Hostesses in the bar or the *mamasan*. More often than not, they will tell you the truth because they know you would be really pissed off if you found out later that they lied. This is one case when experience makes little difference and sometimes it is impossible for even long-term residents to tell. Unless you actually want to be with a ladyboy, be absolutely certain before you do something you may regret.

8
The *Farang*

*"I tried to behave
but there were just too many
other options."*

F oreign visitors to Pattaya come in all shapes, sizes, colours and from every corner of the globe. The one thing first-timers have in common is, no matter how much they have read about Pattaya and in spite of what they have been told, they are usually unprepared for what greets them here. Second-hand information rarely comes close to describing the true picture.

In our modern, mixed-up world, moralists tend to profile the single, male traveller to Asia as a 'sex tourist'. The term is a misnomer and the truth is that no rational person would go to all the trouble and expense of travelling half way around the globe for the sole purpose of indulging in sex. Simple economics: Divide the total amount of money spent on the vacation by the number of sexual encounters to discover it would have been cheaper to stay home and pay a local lady instead.

Sure, the adolescent notion of indulging in 'cheap sex' may be an initial consideration, but it is usually not the main priority or purpose of the trip.

For example, the following letter appeared in the *Bangkok Post* on 30 June 2005:

NEIL HUTCHISON

"The British Foreign Office has just released the results of a survey looking into why young Britons, aged 18-30, go on holiday. The report (which runs to 79 pages) reveals that the most popular reason for going on holiday is "to drink to excess" answered by 75%. A further 8% wanted to take drugs, 28% were looking for casual sex and 5% were looking for a fight (except among respondents from the east of England where 20% wanted a fight).
It reports that the most popular holidays are known as 'home-plus', meaning you get everything you have at home (English food, beer, newspapers, etc) plus a couple of extras such as sunshine and sex."

The results of that survey could easily translate to a response to the question why do people, not only from the UK, visit Pattaya. (Interesting but disturbing to note that almost three times the number of young Britons surveyed preferred getting drunk to having sex. There's a research grant going begging!) This supports the view that 'partying' is a top priority of most holidaymakers. 'Sex' is merely the bait, the sales gimmick, and men who say that is all they are here for are more likely to be seeking the attention and affection of an attractive woman rather than the physical act itself. This is evidenced by the number of men who fall in love; the number who, after only one trip, want to sell up everything back home and move to Thailand; the number who send buckets of money to a wonderful girl they hardly even know and, tragically; those who believe that life has no more meaning if they are unfortunate enough to be discarded by the object of their devotion.

For those people interested in Pattaya's adult entertainment, the best advice is to not take any of the bar scene too seriously, because everything that happens here is just part of a game. Furthermore, it is *their* game, *their* pitch and *their* rules. Beating the Bar Hostesses at their own game is next to impossible so don't waste your precious time and money trying. You may be a big shot in your own country, making decisions every day that affect peoples lives but here you are a babe in the woods. The Bar Hostesses and some resident entrepreneurs have an arsenal of tricks and schemes that you would not believe.

MONEY NUMBER ONE

Some foreign visitors to Amazing Thailand
appear to have left their brain at the airport.

NEIL HUTCHISON

The wiles and guiles that women work,
Dissembled with an outward show,
The tricks and toys that in them lurk,
The cock that treads them shall not know.
William Shakespeare

Observing tourists coming and going, it appears that the *farang* having the best time are the ones who come here for no other reason than to enjoy themselves. Here for a good time, not a long time. They have a wife or girlfriend back home and have no intention of falling in love or becoming romantically involved with a local girl. When they leave, they go home with a smile and a fleeting memory of the faces of the ladies who put it there. No names, just faces.

Then there are those who come here with more money than sense. They throw their money around like drunken sailors and overpay for every service at every opportunity. They think nothing of giving a Beer Bar Hostess 3,000 *baht* for a night or tipping with 100 *baht* notes everywhere they go. They believe that by doing so, they will be loved by all and sundry as well as buy the respect of the local people.

The news for these guys is all bad. Firstly, it requires incredibly low self-esteem to believe the only way to get someone to like you is to throw money at them. Secondly, they are doing a disservice to their fellow *farang* by giving the local population the impression that foreigners are all rich and think nothing of paying exorbitant prices. Thirdly, they gain no points from the locals who quickly realize they are just big, stupid, walking ATMs. Once out of sight, the Bar Hostesses laugh at their stupidity.

The worst at playing the Pattaya game are the guys with the bad, superior attitude. They treat the local Thais like fools, the local expats like trash and call the ladies "whores". Almost without fail, they will get into some serious or costly trouble while they are here on holiday. They get what they deserve, having made no effort to gain the respect of any Thai or expat unfortunate enough to have come into contact with them.

MONEY NUMBER ONE

The Butterfly

> *"Sex without love is a meaningless experience but, as meaningless experiences go, it's pretty damned good!"*
> Woody Allen

Having already stated the idea of a 'sex tourist' is a myth, it may seem inconsistent to report on the nearest equivalent stereotype. In bar culture, a 'butterfly' is the polite term applied to anyone - male or female, tourist or resident, Thai or *farang* - who appears to go through no-strings-attached romantic episodes with a succession of different partners; a sort of love 'em and leave 'em type of person. Therein lies the distinction: a 'sex tourist' travels great distances to satisfy his indulgences whereas a 'butterfly' merely takes advantage of what is being offered around him.

Basically, the idea of noncommittal sex with multiple partners is not a new one. It has been around since man first ventured out of his cave and clobbered the first female (not necessarily human) he happened across. Once satisfied, he would return to his cave, fall asleep and wait until his primal urges rose again. To many men, they were the good old days. In the 21st Century, this caveman scenario is played out daily in the bar areas of Pattaya, Bangkok, Phuket and Chiang Mai. The modern day caveman, however, ventures out of his hotel and uses his wallet, not a club, to score the first Bar Hostess his heart desires.

For wannabe 'butterflies' out there, welcome to the top of the Bar Hostess Shit List. It is amazing that a guy who goes with two or five or ten different ladies in a week is considered the lowest of the low - a 'butterfly', and yet a Bar Hostess who goes with seven different *farang* in as many nights is not. There appears to be bit of a double standard regarding the issue.

Bar Hostesses explain this duplicity easily. When they go with a man, he is not a 'boyfriend' but a 'customer' and it is purely a business arrangement. The nature of the business means she can have as many 'customers' as she chooses. When a *farang* pays her bar fine, the lady becomes his 'girlfriend', a status she retains until *she* decides it is over. Only a 'butterfly' would have more than one 'girlfriend'. Get it?

But be warned! The metamorphosis into a 'butterfly' is not as easy as it sounds, even in a place like Pattaya. This town should be 'butterfly' heaven but, as many novices have discovered, turning into the winged insect is fraught with difficulties.

NEIL HUTCHISON

> ### *TIP*
> *Early in your stay never go with a Hostess from a bar close to your hotel, especially if people in the bar have a clear view of the hotel entrance. Mentally signpost these bars as being off-limits for your butterflying. Start with the bars furthest away from your hotel and work your way back (so to speak). There is no shortage of bars or beautiful ladies to choose from. On the last couple of nights of your holiday it is safe to shop closer to home.*

The reason for this is simple. Due to supply outstripping demand, it is easier to secure the affection of a Bar Hostess than it is to unsecure it. Many Bar Hostesses have a tendency to elevate themselves to the status of 'girlfriend' very quickly and can make more sensitive and caring males feel uncomfortable about playing any farther afield in the future. Experienced men who have done their share of 'butterflying' would likely agree that the further the lady's apartment or bar is from your hotel, the better.

> *The male visitor reported receiving phone calls to his room at all hours of the night. One girl even knocked on his door at 3:00am when he already had another companion in the room. One had her friends staking out the hotel, reporting his movements and the number of female companions he brought to his room. Yet another left him so many messages that he ended up changing hotels just to get some peace. (These things worried him for one other reason - it meant he was obviously being far too generous with the folding stuff.)*

This is not to say that this type of behaviour is common or will happen every time a gentle and delicate Bar Hostess's heart is brutally crushed beneath your Doc Martens, but it can detract from your enjoyment when it does.

> ### *TIP*
> *Even though it may be difficult during high season when most of the hotels are fully booked, it is a good idea to change hotels at some point of your stay to add a bit of variety to your trip and reduce the chances of being bothered by an ex-conquest.*

MONEY NUMBER ONE

When checking out of the hotel, don't tell the receptionist or doorman where you are going. Gossip is the national pastime so should a lady come looking for you, hotel staff will divulge your current whereabouts without hesitation.

A skilled, card-carrying 'butterfly' avoids many problems by never taking a conquest back to his cave. He never divulges his phone number and keeps his dalliances to short sessions in bars providing in-house reclining facilities or hotels charging by the hour. He chooses ladies who are professional and show no interest in anything other than money. That way there is usually no problem if, on his next visit to the bar, he desires the company of another lady working there.

TIP
One guy systematically bar fined every girl working in the bar. His reputation as a 'butterfly' was thus entrenched in stone with all the Hostesses understanding he was not looking for a meaningful relationship. His social standing was one notch above pond scum. To do this effectively, he advised it is important to give each lady the same amount of money because playing favourites will quickly get you into all sorts of trouble.

As in nature, a butterfly's life is short-lived. Flitting from flower to flower, it is a mathematical certainty that eventually one blossom will stand out from the rest. There is nothing more pathetic than a once proud pork swordsman reduced to a blubbering, servile mess through the charms of a lady holding his heart in her gentle hands.

The Cheap Charlie

"Eagles may soar but weasels don't get sucked into jet engines."

Coming in at fourth spot on the Bar Hostess Shit List is the Cheap Charlie, but don't worry about it. Fourth spot is down on the list. Swindlers, cutthroats, rapists and other villains share third spot. Second spot is held by any *farang* who leaves the country without taking down her bank account details.

NEIL HUTCHISON

In general, Pattaya is a cheaper destination than either Bangkok or Phuket so holidaymakers with a limited budget can have a great time here with a little planning. Here is some advice on how to enjoy Pattaya on a shoestring.

1. Accommodation

    If you are a first-timer and have pre-booked your accommodation, you are committed to the travel agent's recommendation. The best thing to do is take note of other places to stay next time. And there will be a next time. This may take some legwork but it will be worth it to find good, cheap accommodation in an area that you like. Rooms with air-conditioning, at around 500 *baht* per night are plentiful. For those staying for a month or more, apartments and guest houses for around 7,000 *baht* per month can be good value. (Prices usually increase during high season.)

2. Food

    For the CC who likes Thai food, it will fit well within budget. European food is relatively expensive. If you like Western food for breakfast, there are a few hotels offering 'all you can eat' breakfasts for around 150 *baht*. The only problem with this is that they only offer it between say 7:00am and 1:00pm. After a few days (and nights) in Pattaya, you will realize that getting out of bed before 1:00pm is not as easy as it sounds.

    In the evening there are buffet dinners offering both Thai and Western food for around 270 *baht*. If you are looking for a free meal at night, take a walk around the bars until you find one having a party. These are easy to spot, as the bar will be festooned with balloons and there will usually be a pig roasting over a portable spit out front. Every night, a bar somewhere will be having a birthday or anniversary party and provide free food for customers. Members of the burgeoning expat community who regularly seek out these parties are branded 'balloon chasers' by the bar owners. So what! If bar owners don't want to attract customers, don't put up balloons and keep the festivities secret.

MONEY NUMBER ONE

3   Transport

As stated in an earlier chapter, *Baht* Buses and motorcycle taxis are currently the cheapest forms of public transport. As stated in an earlier chapter, the ONLY fare on a Baht Bus is 10 *baht* while motorcycle taxis have a minimum fare of 30 *baht*. Central Pattaya is so compact that, unless you have a medical condition or physical problem, walking is an alternative. Late at night, this may be inadvisable or impractical, especially if you have found a charming companion. In general, Thai girls don't walk!

4   Tipping

Tipping is not compulsory in Thailand except in restaurants that add a 'Service Charge' to the bill. No matter how good the food may be, I avoid those places like the plague. Many people find going to a restaurant and four or five different bars each day and leaving a 20 *baht* tip at each place soon adds up. Having said that, it should be pointed out that wages in Thailand for people in the service industry are low so, if you do receive good service, it won't break you to leave a small tip in appreciation.

It should also be pointed out that tipping is only to show appreciation for good service. If you did not get good service, why should you be expected to leave a tip? Do not be afraid to express your disappointment by not leaving any tip. But whatever you do, don't be a smart-arse and leave a 1 *baht* coin as a tip. Leaving 1 *baht* tip is a gross insult to Thais and will not be appreciated, even if you only did it in jest. It is better to leave no tip at all.

5   Drinks

Drinks, of any description, are the most expensive in the discos, nightclubs and Go Go Bars, although quite a few Go Go Bars offer excellent value happy hours with draught beer selling for between 50 and 70 *baht* or two-for-one deals on house spirits. For example, 120 *baht* for two gin tonics or *Sang Som* (Thai rum and a very nice drop) with Coke or soda is quite good value. It is rare for Beer Bars to sell draught beer and the price of small bottled beer averages around 75 *baht*. More and more Beer Bars are advertising 'Happy Hours' in an effort to attract customers and it is a good idea to check them out. For instance, one Beer Bar sells *Sang Som* and mixer for 25 *baht* per glass during happy hour. As a general rule, whenever you see a bar packed with older, badly dressed farang customers sitting by themselves looking sad and miserable, you can bet the booze is cheap.

TIP

Be aware that a 'happy hour' does not mean all drinks are discounted. The local bottled beer may be cheap at 55 baht, but a softdrink could be 70 baht. One Go Go Bar advertised 40 baht draught beer but charged 120 baht for a cup of hot tea.

The cheapest drinks can be purchased from supermarkets and convenience stores but a law enacted in the 1970's, still technically in force and now resurrected forcefully, means alcohol can only be sold between 11:00am and 2:00pm then again between 5:00pm and midnight. Major supermarkets, 7-Elevens and Family Marts will (usually) not sell booze outside those designated times.

6   Female Companionship

Just because you have a limited budget does not mean that you can not enjoy some feminine delights. Beer Bars have the cheapest bar fines, ranging from around 300 *baht*. In Indoor Recreation Lounges it will be 350 to 450 *baht* but that often includes use of a short time room. An overnight guest from a Beer Bar will ask for a minimum of 1,000 *baht*. You may haggle, but do it before you pay the bar fine.

In Soi 6 one afternoon, he asked a girl how much she wanted for a short interlude. She replied 800 baht. Knowing this figure to be outrageous, he told her 500 baht was the going rate. Her next offer was 700 but again he held his ground. Next, she asked for 500 baht plus a 100 baht 'tip'. He refused that as well and, two minutes later, 500 baht was agreed upon.

MONEY NUMBER ONE

9
Farang in Love

City girls have got night life in their eyes
You ask no questions and get told no lies
If you get hurt
Their on the flight again tonight
Tonight
Don't fall in love
Don't fall in love

Great short skirts with no tights
Underneath all there is is lies
Can't you see their cheating all of you
Their no good for you
No good for you
Don't fall in love
Don't fall in love

   * **The Ferrets** were an Australian pop/rock band which formed in 1975 and disbanded in 1979. Their second single, "Don't Fall in Love", was released in 1977 and peaked at No. 2 on the Australian Singles Chart. The lyrics are still very relevant in Pattaya *circa* 2013.

There is a line from another song that goes, "looking for love in all the wrong places." If you are indeed looking for love, it has been suggested that Pattaya may just possibly be the wrongest place on the planet. Nevertheless, many men come here and fall in love, often with the first girl they meet.

NEIL HUTCHISON

Why are many Western men more attracted to Asian ladies than women from their own country? Nobody will disagree that Asian ladies can be very attractive, but so can women in the West. Statistics may show that Asian women, on average, are leaner than Western women and smaller in stature. Perhaps this is the initial attraction, as is evident by the large number of foreign men walking around town holding hands with petite Thai ladies. This subconscious attraction could be attributed to evolutionary factors, but the increasing number of Western males seeking Asian partners means there surely must be more to it than simply hormones.

One possible answer is 'femininity'. Generally speaking, Asian women appear more feminine, enjoy their femininity and exploit their femininity and sensuality to a much larger degree than the modern Western female. The sexual revolution missed Asia for the simple reason it was irrelevant here. Asian women have always been equal in the eyes of the law even though their cultural status remains polarised. However, speaking only in terms of their romantic relationships with men, there is no confusion. Asian women have always had the upper hand because they enjoy being feminine and use it to great advantage.

They don't have a chip on their shoulder. They don't want to dress like men, talk like men or act like men. They don't want to do 'a man's job' even though they know they are capable of it. They like to look beautiful at all times; for themselves, their female friends and the guy they're with. They like to be pampered and flattered by men and don't take it as a patronising, condescending insult if a man opens a door for them. And when a stranger smiles at them, they smile back. Basically, they don't have an inferiority complex nor do they feel they have anything to prove, unlike their counterparts in the West.

No matter what her career choice, a lady in this town knows how to get what she wants from a man. And she can do it with simply a raised eyebrow, a wry smile or a twinkle in her eye. No raised voice, no nagging, no quoting sex discrimination legislation, no ultimatums and no feminist rhetoric. In practical terms, this can be witnessed every day in Pattaya.

> *The young guy in the Baht Bus had to be at least six foot four. He was a tower of rippling muscles, obviously kept himself very fit and could have broken me in two like a pretzel. His crew cut immediately pointed to him being in the military and the tattoo on his shoulder boasting "US Marines – We kill just to keep in practice" (or something macho like that) confirmed*

MONEY NUMBER ONE

it. Sitting beside him was his small, beautiful, sensually-dressed, young Thai girlfriend who would have weighed no more than forty kilograms (ninety pounds) wringing wet. Their conversation, beginning with the rough and tough marine, went like this:

"I'm sorry honey. I only said hello to her, nothing else."
(Quietly ignored by his girlfriend.)
"Oh, shoot, sweetheart, I swear I've never seen her before ... I was just being polite."
(A slight expressionless glance and raised eyebrow from his girlfriend.)
"Honey ... you know you're the only one for me. I love my little pookie."
(Another seductive turn of his girlfriend's head, this time with the hint of a sexy "Go on ... I'm listening" smile. After brief eye contact she turns her head away abruptly, making sure her long silky hair flails against his naked shoulder.)
"I promise I'll never do it again ... I'll only have eyes for you, pumpkin."

That true story still makes me nauseous. If only his buddies in the p'toon could have seen him in operation. The point is, that little Thai lady used her femininity and female guiles to bring down her Goliath. No shouting, no squabble, no "men are scum" argument and no threats. Asian women know all too well you can catch more flies with honey than with vinegar.

Another answer could be that, in some cases, a Western man may have spent so many years being rejected by women in his own country that he cannot resist the first female who shows an interest in him, not helped by the fact she is probably beautiful and half his age. Perhaps he is simply lonely and the ease at which female companionship can be found in Pattaya overwhelms him. For many Western men, a Bar Hostess indicating a desire to be intimate with him and the subsequent act itself sends him a message that she loves him. He overlooks the fact that a financial transaction also took place, justifying it by saying the money was his 'gift' to her rather than her 'fee'. He blindly forgets that having sex for money is her job and is completely different to having sex with someone she loves.

Perhaps the answer lies with Western culture where, for centuries, moralists have been preaching that 'love' and 'sex' are equated. Religious zealots scream that sex is an act of love and should come as a result of the love. 'Love' is an integral part of, and should always precede, 'sex'. Once the honeymoon is over, some married men become further conditioned by their wives to believe that sex is a reward for good deeds rather than a spontaneous event to be enjoyed by both husband and wife. "If you mow the lawn, clean out the shed and build me a cupboard, you might just get lucky tonight." Like a trained seal, he does his chores and waits to receive his 'prize' at the end of the day. Even the term 'get lucky' is used to belittle and intimidate men. Once in Pattaya, he discovers that here, sex is simply another bodily function which does not necessarily have anything to do with love.

A problem arises when a supposedly intelligent man, after half a century of bad luck or poor judgement where women are concerned, travels halfway round the world and, within the space of five minutes, believes he has the greatest stroke of luck in finding his perfect lady. In every case, he is misguided by the belief that she is the only one for him. In spite of warnings from expats and well-meaning friends to take things slowly and play the field until he learns more about the place, he convinces himself she is 'different' and he can't live without her. He also forgets a golden rule:

"In relationships of the heart, the power is held by the one who loves the least."

Before falling hopelessly in love with a Bar Hostess, there are some important things to consider. Remember that Pattaya is a city of extremes where it is almost impossible to find a 'middle ground' or 'happy medium'. The word 'love' is often thrown around with such abandon to render it as meaningless as ordering a plate of fish and chips. Then, on occasion, it can invoke the most powerful emotions and, in extreme cases, lead to tragic consequences.

"Remember, no matter how good she looks, some other guy is sick and tired of putting up with her shit!"

MONEY NUMBER ONE

But what about those relationship-seeking men who conclude that the bar scene is not the best place to search for a mate. After several negative experiences with bar girls he may make efforts to distance himself from any girl tainted by prostitution, branding them all hookers and liars.

There is continual debate within the expat community over the 'good girl/bad girl' argument. The jury is still out on the issue but, in the book *The Fool is Back!*, I made the following observations:

"He may decide to seek out, woo and marry a Thai girl from a respectable middle class family or, even better, one from a respectable upper class (i.e. wealthy) family. The catch is, with few exceptions, Thai ladies from the respectable middle and upper classes only want to marry Thai men from the same, or higher, classes. They are not likely to fall for an old, divorced foreigner of moderate means. Her family will be reluctant to allow her to get involved with foreign men because they are aware there is little future in the relationship.

"He is left with finding a partner from the working class or from the less affluent areas of Thailand. There are plenty to choose from but these girls are extremely shy with strangers and more so with foreigners. Unless he speaks the language he is not likely to get very far. If he finds a girl who interests him he cannot treat her as he would a bar girl. He must woo her and win her and her family. He must do this properly and in the traditional Thai way. This means no sex or public signs of affection for a considerable period of the courtship. He must always respect her family's wishes and take things very slowly. Given that the guy is probably old to begin with, he may not have the patience or the time to go through these motions."

It is possible to find 'good girls' working in the bars just as it is possible to find 'bad girls' stocking shelves in supermarkets. It is her overall character that matters because her needs, desires and expectations don't change in accordance with her career choices.

Whether she works in a bar or a 7-Eleven, there is no lady here walking around with "Pick me – I'm a good one!" tattooed on her forehead. Although most things are possible, newcomers should never attempt to find the girl of their dreams until they have at least become very familiar with the place and Thai ways. A little restraint in the beginning will prove invaluable later. Experienced *farang* will tell you that the attrition rate when searching for the right partner is astronomical. In layman's terms, this means you may have to have to kiss a lot of frogs before you find your princess.

Early Danger Signs

For any *farang* thinking about entering a long-term relationship with a lady he recently met in a bar, there is one major flaw; *she* did not choose him. He selected her to be his mate but what if she would never have picked him had the roles been reversed? What if she doesn't actually like him? She accepts the attention and whatever else he offers but what if her heart is not really in it?

There are some subtle but recognizable early warning signs to look out for. Statistically, the following Bar Hostess types have a poor track record when it comes to maintaining serious relationships:

1. Those wearing an abundance of gold chains, bracelets etc.
Basically, a Pattaya Bar Hostess cannot afford to buy a lot of expensive jewellery unless she has a *farang* sponsor or many *farang* boyfriends. These girls are very 'street-wise', demand more money for their time and know exactly how to extract every extra $ from men. Unless your name is Bill Gates and you whisk her away from Pattaya to live happily ever after, she is not likely to give up her other 'friends' for you.

2. Those who tell you that they live alone.
Apart from the obvious financial obstacles to living alone, there are some other things you should understand. Most, but not all, Bar Hostesses who tell you they live alone are possibly being less than forthright.

Every afternoon his girlfriend would return to her room to change clothes, do her washing, then meet him back at his hotel at 8.00pm. After a month or so, he told her "I'll come with you. I want to see your apartment." Well, it was like he had just run over her grandmother and raped her cat. "You can not come my apartment. I never take farang to my apartment." With that, she walked out.

Next day she turned up at the hotel, apologized in her insincere way and said that if he still wanted to see her apartment, he could. It did not take an Einstein to work out that whatever it was that she did not want him to see had now been removed and her room had been made 'safe' to visit. He went anyway.

MONEY NUMBER ONE

"Hello 'ello 'ello!"

To cut a long story short, he was always suspicious after that and would turn up at her apartment without warning. One day he noticed she was in a particular hurry to get him to leave. She had just had a shower, was dressing very quickly and the bathroom door was closed. Before she ushered him out of her room, he made an excuse to use the bathroom. In spite of her protestations, he opened the door. Guess what he found? There was a stark naked Thai man hiding behind the door. It turned out he was her boyfriend/pimp who she had been living with for three years. He was a motorcycle taxi driver who would also send her 'customers' from time to time. He was living with her rent-free and enjoying the proceeds of her hard work.

That story is not unique, and regrettably, many such girls spoil it for the few genuine cases.
TIP
If you are really keen on a girl who says she lives by herself, then check out her apartment. Don't give her advance warning. If she makes any excuse whatsoever as to why you can't come with her, suspect something is not right. Do not let her make any phone calls or talk to any of her friends on the way and be very suspicious of any delaying tactics. Unless you have her enthusiastic agreement, she has something to hide.

3   Those who have been working in a bar for more than three months. The longer she has been working in a bar the more conditioned she becomes. She is taught every trick in the book by her co-workers and 'Money Number One' gets burned into her brain. Remember, no girl who comes to work bar is from the social elite of Thailand. She is often just a simple girl from Wherethefuckaburi who has no job at home and so comes to earn money to support herself, perhaps her child and definitely her family. Her formal education will be limited.

She will quickly establish friendships with the other girls and learn many skills of the trade from them. She may also have a number of regular boyfriends. For hardened Bar Hostesses, it is not the quality, generosity or kindness of her one *farang* boyfriend which measures her prestige among her peers but the quantity of generous *farang* boyfriends she can accumulate.

MONEY NUMBER ONE

One Bar Hostess quit work once she had accumulated three farang boyfriends, each from a different country. Two of them sent her 10,000 baht per month and the other sent her 20,000 baht. This girl did not need to work any more because she took home 40,000 baht (US$1,300) each month. She personally knew three other girls who received in excess of 100,000 baht per month in exactly the same fashion. Should two or all of the boyfriends turn up in Pattaya at the same time, she simply attends to the most generous one and puts the other(s) on hold.

How can you tell if a lady has been working in a bar for a long period of time? On arrival, the vast majority of the girls will not be able to speak a word of English. They are, however, very intelligent and quick learners. Those who have been working bars for more than three months are easy to spot because they will know some degree of English. As a general rule of thumb, the more fluent in English they are, the longer they have been exposed to it. And in spite of what they may say, they don't get a lot of exposure to the English language back home in the province.

What is the point of getting a girlfriend who can't speak your language? If your intention is to settle down with a long-term girlfriend, then it is a trade-off; a compromise. As we all know, there are other ways to communicate besides talking. Once you have won her heart and removed her from the bar scene, you can teach her to speak English while, at the same time, you should learn to speak Thai.

4   Those who appear to have a 'brother' or any male 'relative' hanging around or constantly in the picture.

Why? Because, in spite of her assurances, the guy is probably not her brother. Most often he is her boyfriend or husband. Don't bother trying to check it out by asking her friends because they will never tell you the truth.

I have it on good authority (confirmed by other Thais) that in moral Thai society an adult, unmarried Thai female will NEVER share accommodation with an adult, unmarried male relative. It is socially forbidden. If she is married and her husband is present or if he is married and his wife is present, it is OK, but a Thai brother and sister sharing an apartment is impossible.

5   Those who have a gallery of tattoos all over their body and/or excessive body piercing apart from simple ear rings. Especially if she sports a tattoo with the words "I love John" and your name is Fred. Any person - male, female, Thai or *farang* - who would have the name of someone else tattooed on their body has sawdust for brains.

The girl sitting behind the bar had the words, "Property of Johnny" tattooed in a circle on her shoulder. I asked her if she knew what it meant. No idea. I then asked where Johnny was. She said they were finished and he had gone back to his home country. At the time, Johnny obviously thought it was a great joke but now that poor girl has to wear her offensive graffiti forever.

6   Those deeply attached to their mobile phones.
The Bar Hostesses of Pattaya have embraced the cellular communication revolution with unbridled enthusiasm. Phone prices have dropped substantially so even new arrivals can afford a basic model. It is almost impossible to find a Bar Hostess who does not have at least one mobile phone. Nevertheless, be wary of any lady who seems to have an obsession with her phone, making and receiving an inordinate amout of calls at all times of the day or night. It could indicate that her cellular 'friends' are far more important to her than your company.

The Bar Hostess was talking to her farang lover on her mobile. She spoke good English. Her current boyfriend sitting beside her was German and did not speak good English. Otherwise, he would have heard her tell the (absent) love-of-her-life how much she missed him and how she was waiting for him to come back to her.

Without taking this to the point of paranoia, try calling her at random times during the night. Insist that she answers when you do call her. Don't listen to excuses about flat batteries, broken phones or "I left the phone in my apartment while I went shopping." Thais call each other at any time of the day or night so be VERY suspicious if ever

MONEY NUMBER ONE

"No, darling, I never go with other *farang*.
Only wait for you."

her phone is switched off. Keep note of all missed calls you make and look for any pattern developing. If she calls you, never answer her immediately. Wait at least thirty minutes before calling her back. Sometimes a person up to mischief will make an unscheduled phone call to reduce the risk of the other person calling them later.

When she was alone in Pattaya, one Bar Hostess carried three mobile phones in her purse; one for each boyfriend. When 'Bill' was in town, she only carried his assigned phone with her and hid the other two away in her room. When she was with 'Fred' she carried his assigned phone and hid the other two. The same went for 'Sam'. This meant there was no chance either of the other two guys would call while she was with the third. It also meant if any boyfriend checked her phone for suspicious numbers or messages, there was nothing to find. Whenever she got time to herself, she would check for any missed calls or messages on the other phones and call them back if necessary. This was one very organised lady.

Insist that her phone is her responsibility and you will accept no excuse about it being broken, lost or stolen. It has been reported that some girls have given away or sold their phone knowing full well their *farang* boyfriends will replace it, usually with a better (more expensive) model.

Financial Support

There is no such thing as a free lunch and this is particularly true of Bar Hostess-*farang* unions. Many men who have had long-term relationships with Bar Hostesses will confirm that it can be a more expensive exercise than remaining a single, devil-may-care butterfly. (In fact this not only applies to Bar Hostesses but to women everywhere, as I'm sure many married men will testify.)

In the case of a Thai lady, an added problem arises because of a conflict of cultures. Usually, when a Western couple get married or move in together, their responsibility is limited to taking care of each other. Sometimes it can extend to supporting any dependant children. In Thailand, children are morally obligated to help support their parents once they come of age and have the capicity to do so. The overwhelming evidence is that

MONEY NUMBER ONE

daughters take this obligation more seriously than sons. Certainly, there are exceptions, but a foreign boyfriend must come to terms with this if he wants to sustain a more permanent relationship.

Even though this obligation to help support her parents is part of her upbringing, it is *her* obligation, not yours. If you have the funds you should be benevolent, but it does not mean you have to instantly become the walking ATM for her whole family and come to their financial rescue any time one of them needs a few *baht*. In an e-mail sent to the popular Stickman website (www.stickmanweekly.com), a Thai lady wrote:

> *"We (Thai women) test if we can respect you by stretching the boundaries, especially early in the relationship. We are possessive, jealous, spending recklessly your money, screaming, sulking, crying, throwing things at you, etc. If you let us do it one time, we learn we can do it. If you let us keep doing it, we learn we don't need to respect you and we have the upper hand. You need to be consistent on what is allowed and what is not in our relationship. All those manipulative tools are what we've used and worked with Thai men. Teach us that they don't work in a relationship with you."*

The first thing a man will do once he thinks he has found the girl of his dreams in a bar is tell her to stop working. It is in our nature to do so. We all want our girlfriend to be kind, loving, honest and faithful. We certainly don't want her sleeping with other men. Well gentlemen, there is good news and bad news. For her part, the good news is that the 'kind' and 'loving' requirements can be met, in most cases, with a little patience. The bad news is the 'honest' and 'faithful' criteria will require a more substantial effort from both of you.

The moment you ask your lady to stop working bar, she will agree. In her very next breath she will ask something like, "How much you give me money for food and for Mama." This is a reasonable request because that money is to compensate for the lack of income she was getting from the bar work.

In the case of the two of you moving in together on a permanent basis, the next section is somewhat of a moot point. But in the case where you will be absent from Thailand for long periods of time during the year, there are serious considerations.

Being an Absent Boyfriend

For those men required to work at jobs around the world or with commitments in their home country taking them out of Thailand for long periods, supporting a Thai girlfriend gets complicated.

On the financial side, if the idea is that she remains here while he goes to work and sends her money every month, he needs to set the ground rules from the start to ensure his money is being used for fruitful endeavours.

Her monthly rent and utilities will be around 3,000 *baht* if she shares a room with other girls. Apart from extraordinary expenses (sick buffalo etc.), her cost of living will be at least an additional 3,000 *baht*. In 2013, the minimum amount requested is 10,000 *baht* per month which seems to be the accepted first offer but may not be enough to ensure her faithfulness. Don't forget, she will also be sending money home to her family. Some ladies who have a child/children from a previous relationship will also be sending money for the child's schooling. Education may be free in Thailand but books and uniforms are not.

Before you tell her to stop work, agree to send her money or do anything else, please think about it very seriously. You must sit down with her and ascertain exactly what she requires each month to satisfy her *reasonable* financial commitments. Once her monthly budget is known, you must see if it fits with your own financial circumstances. If it is above what you can afford then perhaps you should re-think the relationship.

Pattaya Bar Hostesses don't understand the word 'budget' so don't try to design one for her because once you are absent there is little chance she will stick to it. Her family and friends will be putting pressure on her and there are just too many other *farang* in Pattaya presenting too many temptations for her to make some extra cash.

The following is a fictitious letter comprising various reasons given by the Bar Hostesses to their *farang* boyfriends as to why he should send her (more) money. Each reason has been used individually many times and the list is by no means complete. Once you give a Bar Hostess your postal address or e-mail address, you may receive a letter or e-mail, not exactly the same, but with similar intent.

MONEY NUMBER ONE

Dear (farang)* insert your name here
I love you and miss you too much. Now I have problem. I tell you before that buffalo me sick. Now it die. Fall down dead in middle of rice field. Unfortunately, when it fall, it land on Papa and break his leg in three places. Now he can not work. Brother me make stretcher from bamboo she take from roof of house. Then roof collapse and rain get in house. She take Papa to hospital on motorcycle. She have accident coming home. Run into police car. Brother me to blame. Police say he have to pay big money. Motorcycle OK. Police car kaput. Now give Mama have heart problem. Doctor say she need triple bypass. I not understand what is. He say you understand. Up to now I only work cashier in bar and not go with man. I wait for you come back Pattaya. If you will not help me I have to go with many many many many more farang to pay bill. The old people in my village in Wherethefuckaburi think that it is all your fault. If you had send me money to buy medicine for sick buffalo when I ask you, then it not die, Papa not break leg, house still have roof, brother not ride into Police car and Mama not have heart problem. Please send for me 200,000 baht for my bank account. Papa fix: 10,000 New roof: 30,000 New Police car: 100,000 Mama fix: 50,000. I take off 2,000 baht for sell buffalo meat but have to pay more hospital bill for 24 people have problem eat contaminated meat - 12,000 baht. I not know money Australia but my friend me say it about 30.59875 baht. This mean you send me 10,000 dollar Australia. Little bit money for you. I love you too much.
Lek

On the emotional side, let me first say that the expression, "absence makes the heart grow fonder" is a total load of crap.

There are three ways to handle prolonged separation from your Thai lady. Firstly, you can choose to live in a fool's paradise by accepting her at her word and looking the other way when suspicion or jealousy raise their ugly heads. Some men employ this 'head buried in the sand' strategy very successfully.

Secondly, you can stress yourself out to the point of a stroke by trying to maintain a continuous guard on her in an attempt to keep her on the straight and narrow.

One absent boyfriend was so concerned that his girlfriend would go back on the game, he asked his farang friends in Pattaya to visit her bar from time to time and report to him if she was still working. They refused, like most sensible expats would. It is not their job to play 'spy' and what if they reported she was still working? What could the distant boyfriend do about it? Whether he broke up with her or forgave her, his life would still become miserable.

The third option is to tell her that, while you are away, you will only support her if she moves out of Pattaya. She can either go back to stay at her home in the country or move to a place of your choosing. If she refuses to leave, then perhaps she is just another gold-digger and the solution would be not to waste any more time on her. If she agrees, you should then ensure she moves all her belongings while you are there to supervise. Do not accept her 'promise' to undertake the move once you are off working. She is certain to come up with excuse as to why she cannot move house this month.

If all goes well and she does leave Pattaya, then you can pat yourself on the back. You have become a member of a small club of foreigners who have won the heart of a Bar Hostess. Now, you have to make good all of your promises to her. Her cost of living at home or in the countryside will be no less than in Pattaya. Her needs may in fact be higher because there she will be regarded as a source of cash by all her friends, relatives and neighbours. Tell her that is not an option, and her allowance will not be increased to take care of any local parasites.

You must also discuss what she is going to do to fill in her time. Country life can become mundane for a girl who has lived the daily excitement of Pattaya. Keeping her occupied may involve paying for her to attend an English or computer course or perhaps setting up a small business for her to be involved in. Don't expect the business to make any money for you (read Chapter 12), so don't go overboard.

At this point there are so many things that could happen and so many variables that you will have to play it by ear. Make sure to visit her or bring her to visit you as often as possible. Don't just come to Thailand once a year for your annual vacation. When you visit her, it is a good idea not to tell her when you are arriving. It is amazing the amount of information you can get when you turn up unexpectedly. It is an excellent way of testing her honesty and loyalty. At least it will keep her on her toes.

MONEY NUMBER ONE

For the man more or less permanently residing in Thailand, he and the lady will be living together so it is relatively easy to keep track of her movements and oversee her spending. By taking care of all day to day living expenses, he can ensure the money he gives her for herself and to send home is reasonable and well within *his* budget.

Going on 'Holiday'

So far, a lot of ink has been spent trying to convince you just how much Thais love Thailand. This is not to say that they don't mind getting out of the place from time to time, especially if someone else is paying. Good girls go to Heaven, Pattaya girls go everywhere. Getting the object of your love-lust to agree to go on holiday with you is not a problem. Just ask. It is almost certain her answer will be an emphatic "Yes!" If you have been going with her for a long time (more than three consecutive nights), she may not even wait for you to ask.

Once you have pencilled your lady in as being a long-term prospect, a good idea is to take her with you on trips within Thailand initially. The main reason behind this strategy will become obvious later. She will only be too happy to show off her wonderful country and can be your interpreter while you can assess how good a 'traveller' she is. A visit to her home village is a 'must' and this is dealt with in detail in Chapter 10. Many *farang* have reported that their side-trip to Chiang Mai, Ko Chang or Ko Samui was made more enjoyable in the company of their girlfriend. A relative few have said their trip was a nightmare due to constant complaints from the lady. As a result, they felt it wise to discontinue the relationship or, at least, discontinue travelling with her.

Assuming she is a good travelling companion, taking her on trips to other countries presents a different challenge. She may already have a passport but, if she does not, getting a passport for her is neither difficult nor expensive. She simply takes her Thai ID Card to the Passport Office located on the fifth floor of Central Plaza Bang Na on Sukhumvit Road in south eastern Bangkok and pays a fee of 1,000 *baht*. She can come back and collect the passport herself or, for an extra 40 *baht*, the passport will be mailed to her in less than a week.

It is advisable to take her on a holiday to another ASEAN country first, because Thais usually don't need to obtain a prior visa. Taking a Thai companion on holiday with you to Vietnam, Hong Kong, Singapore, Malaysia or the Philippines should not present any problems. Laos and

Cambodia operate differently and, like you, she will probably need to obtain a visa. Cambodia actually allows Thais from the border provinces to enter the country for a short period using only their ID cards but they must exit the country the same way. Check first.

For trips farther afield, understand that most Thais do not like cold weather which, to them, is anything under 28°C (85°F). If you are considering taking her to England or Europe in winter, then prepare yourself for constant complaining. One week of cold weather and she will want to go home. One week of her constant moaning and you will be happy to send her home.

If you decide to take her home to meet your mother, she will almost certainly have to obtain a visa. This is when you may experience difficulties depending on which country you are taking her to. I don't pretend to know anything about obtaining a foreign visa for a Thai national but I have seen the criteria set out by the Australian government and, according to American and UK friends who have been through the process, the requirements of their respective governments are similar.

In general, the criteria she needs to satisfy *may* include, but are not limited to:

1. Must have evidence of funds to support a visit of the proposed duration.
2. Must show a level of personal, financial, employment and other commitments which may provide inducement to return to country of usual residence.
3. Must be no circumstances in her country of usual residence which may provide inducement NOT to return.
4. Must be evidence of having previously complied with visa conditions of (your country) or any other country. (*This is why I recommended taking her to another ASEAN country first.*)
5. Must be no inconsistencies in claims made by the applicant and those made by any other person supporting the application.
6. The person or persons supporting the application must not have supported other applicants who travelled to (your country) and breached conditions of entry or undertakings made in connection with their entry.
7. Must be no likelihood that the applicant will engage in employment in (your country).
8. Must be no lack of credibility in terms of character and conduct.

MONEY NUMBER ONE

9   The information provided in the context of the application must not be false or designed to mislead.
10   Must be sufficient evidence of credible and bonafide plans. *(Make up a detailed itinerary to cover each day of the holiday.)*

TIP
If you have only known the lady for a couple of months, you will experience problems getting her a visa. Your embassy in Bangkok can require both of you to attend private interviews. You may be asked to show proof (photos etc.) that you have been together for more than just a few days. She will be asked questions about your relationship and if she doesn't know things such as your last name or your date of birth there could be problems. At one embassy, a zealous interviewer asked to see her mobile phone then went through all the telephone numbers and text messages and questioned who they were from.

It may seem obvious but, once you obtain her visa, organize it so that you accompany her on the flight. Do not just leave her with a refundable air ticket or the money to buy a ticket and then tell her that you will meet her at some foreign airport. The reasons for this are threefold:

(a)   If you leave her a refundable ticket or the money for a ticket, you can be certain that before it comes time for her to fly off into your arms, she will have found better uses for the money. You will be told of some 'emergency' or family crisis that required the immediate influx of (your) funds in order to solve. Send more money.

(b)   She will have to fill out the immigration and customs forms on the plane. Even if she can speak English, her written English skills will be nonexistent. The Immigration Form has a space for 'Home Address'. Even though she has a valid visa, the very second she writes 'Pattaya' in that space, Immigration Officers all over the world hear alarm bells. She should put her actual home address in the province. The problems do not end there. What does she write in the space marked 'Occupation'? It would be inappropriate to tell you to lie to the lovely Immigration people (in case one is reading this now), but it would seem not a good idea that she write 'Bar Hostess'.

(c)   She loves Thai food. The thought of not eating Thai food for seven or more days is simply too torturous for her to contemplate. She will therefore decide to bring some of her favourite food and essential ingredients with her. You can tell her not to until you are blue in the face but it is no use. As well as a problem with Immigration, she now has a problem with Customs. The sniffer-dogs at the airport will do backflips when they get a whiff of your ladylove's luggage. You should supervise the packing of her suitcase and throw out any items which may cause the ire of Customs Officers.

On the subject of what you cannot take with you on a plane or into a foreign country, there are some things which you may not be aware of. For instance:

1. It is illegal to take some Buddhist artifacts and genuine Thai antiques out of Thailand.
2. Anything which could be considered a weapon, even if it can be purchased quite legally on the streets of Pattaya, cannot be taken into many countries. e.g. throwing stars, flick knives even if concealed as cigarette lighters, battery-operated stun guns and replica firearms even if they are made of plastic or rendered incapable of being fired, lazer pointers and those battery-powered bug-zappers that look like squash rackets.
3. Certain pharmaceuticals such as anobolic steroids. Should you be found carrying 50 packets of Viagra tablets back home, even if you purchased them from a pharmacy and have a receipt, you better also have a good excuse!
4. Entering Australia for example, all foodstuffs and anything made of wood, plant or animal material must be declared. Anything made from an 'endangered' animal or plant will be confiscated. Any 'copy' goods such as DVDs and CDs, or fake brand name clothing, perfume and handbags will be looked at closely. The latest information is you may get away with being in possession of only one or two items, but if you have say 100 copy DVDs then be prepared to incur a substantial fine and have them confiscated.

The guy dutifully declared the large, magnificently carved teak elephant he was carrying to the female Australian Customs Officer. He was so proud of having bargained for almost an hour with the seller in a Bangkok market. She examined it for a moment before telling him it was OK to take through. As he

MONEY NUMBER ONE

carefully packed it back in his suitcase, she smiled and, in a matter-of-fact voice, informed him it was made of plastic.

5.   Due to increased security measures, cigarette lighters are no longer allowed on flights into the United States (and quite a few other countries).

At Bangkok airport, the x-ray detected the 100 novelty, refillable cigarette lighters in his suitcase he was taking home to give away as gifts. The lighters themselves were not a problem but the airport security staff made him empty each one of gas before letting him through. It took him 45 minutes and he almost missed his flight.

6.   It should go without saying that possession of pornography of any description is illegal.

A US citizen returning to the States had his suitcase randomly searched by US Customs. In it they found his expensive camera and a half dozen packets of photo negatives. The Customs guy went through every strip of negatives, holding each one up to the light, in search of anything resembling pornography. The photos were all touristy stuff and there was no problem, but the passenger was delayed for over an hour while his undeveloped holiday snaps were closely scrutinized.

Correspondence

Marriage counsellors preach that communication is the most important part of any successful relationship. For mere males, experience teaches us that it is difficult enough for a man to communicate with a woman of his own nationality let alone one who can't speak his language. All women seem to speak a different language to men. A women may understand the words alright, but string a few together into a coherent sentence and she puts a whole new meaning to it. For instance, a man telling his wife, "Sorry I'm late darling, but there was a terrible accident on the freeway and we were held up for two hours. I tried to call you but the battery in my mobile was dead", is interpreted as, "I stayed out to have a few beers with my mates because I don't love you and don't care how long it took you to prepare dinner." Communicating with a foreign girlfriend is even trickier.

NEIL HUTCHISON

He flew back home for a six month working stint. His girlfriend, Lek, had come to the airport to see him off before heading home to **Korat** *(where else?) to take care of mama and papa while he was away. Before boarding, he took a photo of the plane to finish off a roll of film. After about a week, he wrote a letter to Lek enclosing some of the photos he had taken. On the back of the photograph of the plane, he wrote 'My plane' in Thai, with the help of a Thai-English dictionary.*

Some weeks later he received an e-mail from Lek. It was in English and contained the usual 'love you' and 'miss you' stuff. What was really amusing was her comment on the photo. "It is not really your plane, is it? It is the plane of Thai Airways International. You don't have to lie to me, darling."
Imagine the commotion the photo must have caused at chez Lek.
"Does he really own a plane?"
"Is he very rich?"
"No, he is a lying bastard. That is a Thai Airways plane."

It proved just how difficult it is to translate exact English meaning into Thai. A native English speaker, reading 'my plane' on the back of the photograph would immediately realize the meaning as 'this is the plane that I flew on'. When he translated 'my plane' into Thai, it came across as 'the plane that belongs to me'.

Every relationship endures periods of separation. Whether it be for one week or six months, maintaining the relationship for the time the two of you are apart requires frequent communication. The telephone is obviously the best method of keeping in contact but international calls can be expensive. For those with access to computers, video linking through Skype is free although the quality of reception can vary depending on location and how many other users are on line. Writing a letter is cheap but it takes too long to arrive and some never arrive at all. More and more Bar Hostesses rely on e-mails and Facebook to keep track of their overseas boyfriends. Both are cheap and instantaneous.

She won't write to you in Thai. The Internet offers free translation software (Google, Bing, Babylon etc) but the results are far from impressive. Sometimes the gobbledegook that comes out is unintelligible.

MONEY NUMBER ONE

I wrote a short English sentence and used Google for the translation. I then copied the Thai and pasted it into Bing. The resulting English translation was nothing like I had written. I then tried Babylon and the result was completely different. In frustration I pasted the Thai back into Google where, surprise surprise, the English was different again, even though it was the same Thai that Google had originally translated from English.

She could draft the letter in Thai and pay for it to be translated into English by a translation service where, for a fee (upwards of 30 *baht* per page), they will translate it for her. Some Internet Cafes will translate and type the e-mail for her as part of their service. It does not matter if the lady is not computer literate.

Sounds simple doesn't it? The problem arises because many of the translators are Thai nationals who have learned English. They have learned very simple English and, whereas it would be impudent to suggest any Thai person is capable of making a mistake, they do. They not only make errors translating her Thai into English, but also in translating your e-mail into Thai.

Using the K.I.S.S. (Keep It Simple Stupid) Principle, here are some suggestions for writing to your girlfriend:

1   No colloquialisms.
The Thai manager of the hotel was in a highly confused state. He had just received an e-mail from a guy who wished to change the dates of his booking. The e-mail began, "Sorry to be such a bloody pest...". The manager had no idea what the writer meant by that. His first thought was the guy was complaining that the hotel was full of vermin bleeding all over the place.

2   No slang.
"This bloke is a good mate."
Australians and many English people will understand exactly what is meant by that statement. In most other parts of the world, it may confuse the reader. The word 'bloke' may not appear in smaller dictionaries and 'mate' may not have its slang meaning mentioned. The statement may make no sense to Thais at all.

3   Short sentences with only one verb in each.
In a letter to a Bar Hostess he once wrote that she was, "so beautiful I can't believe you would not have many boyfriends." (Truly sickening stuff.) *Her friend called him from Pattaya and told him that his girlfriend was very upset when she got the letter and had cried uncontrollably. He could not understand why until he got back and read the translation provided for her. It read "You are beautiful. I don't believe you. You have many boyfriends." It took a lot of slow talking to assure her that was not what he had meant.*

4   Short, simple common words.
"I am continually overwhelmed by joyous anticipation of our impending reunion" may make sense to your English professor but will only confuse a Thai Bar Hostess. Try "I can not wait to see you again" or "I miss you" instead.

Once you have finished drafting your letter, read it back. If it sounds rather childish, then you have succeeded. Those are the easiest letters to translate and there is a good chance the meaning will not be lost.

10
Her Family

One of the standard, sick and derogatory jokes among foreign Pattayaholics is they are all searching for a girlfriend who is an orphan with no friends or living relatives. She is what these pathetic men are looking for but, by all accounts, nobody has found yet. If they have, they have kept very quiet about it. The reason for the needle-in-a-haystack search will become obvious to you once you have established a long-term relationship (more than three consecutive nights) with your dream girl.

Western comedians obtain much of their material from relationships with in-laws, as evidenced by the numerous 'mother-in-law' jokes doing the rounds. This is not so in wonderful Thailand where the family unit is sacred and intra-family relationships are always of the highest and most respected order. Tasteless jokes about in-laws are forbidden and the extended Thai family unit is the envy of the rest of the world.

NEIL HUTCHISON

Visiting Her Family

At some point in your relationship, you may be invited to visit her family back in the province. This is a great honour and an opportunity not to be missed. Remember though, Pattaya is not typical of Thailand and your behaviour in Pattaya can not be translated to your behaviour in rural Thailand. There are many excellent, sincere books on Thai etiquette, with perhaps the best being *Thailand Fever* by Chris Pirazzi and Vitida Vasant. This book explains how you should behave and the reasons why her family acts the way they do. You would be well advised to read up a little before departing fun town. If you are not invited to meet her family, the reason could be one or more of the following:

1. She may not have the same level of commitment to the relationship that you do. As astute and intuitive as Thai ladies are, she may not see the relationship as having much future. Or, she may not really like you.
2. She has taken too many *farang* boyfriends home already. There are social restrictions on the number of different *farang* she can take home to meet the family. She may get away with two but never more than three. This is because, when a *farang* arrives at her village, he is the talking point of the whole place. Everyone, and that means everyone, will come out to see the *farang* that *Lek* has brought home. She may be able to explain (lie) why this *farang* is not the same as the last one she was with but, after the third one, she will probably lose face and be known as what we in the West refer to as a 'cheap girl'. This is social suicide for both her and her family.
3. She may be embarrassed because she thinks her family is *jon* [poor] in relation to the lifestyle she perceives you as leading in your own country.
4. She does not get along with her parents (rare) or her family disapprove of her choice of career in Pattaya.
5. She has a Thai husband at home and it would be too difficult to hide him from you, especially if she has children. It would also mean a loss of face for her husband if you showed up.

Once invited to go to her home, be warned that it can be very EXPENSIVE. By all means, go. It is a great experience and a good break from the rigours of bar life but be prepared both emotionally and financially.

MONEY NUMBER ONE

Your hand and your wallet may begin a new, committed and continuous relationship. They will not be separated for more than five minutes.

There are several ways to get to her home. By bus, train, hire car with driver or hire a car and drive yourself. The bus or train (if available) is by far the cheapest method but it is long, arduous and not very convenient as buses and trains sometimes leave or arrive at odd hours. Your lady will know all about the bus because that is her means of transport each time she returns home for a visit. Hiring a car or minibus with a driver is easy, much more convenient and comfortable, but obviously more expensive. If you have the confidence (plus a valid Thai or International Drivers License and comprehensive insurance) to hire a car and drive yourself, remember that even though the roads in Thailand are excellent and most Thai road users are breathtaking, some unskilled drivers forfeit caution for speed.

Rolling up outside her home in a nice, shiny car is much more socially acceptable than arriving at Mama's house by bus and tuk-tuk. Your lady will be delighted.

TIP
Do not get sucked into taking any of her friends with you. On his first trip up country, his lady asked if she could bring her friend along. Being a kind and generous farang, he agreed. The Thai language does not have plurals, so when she said "friend" she really meant "friends". He ended up with five girls squeezed into the car. Guess who pays? The second time, he put his foot down and said only one friend was allowed. This turned out to be almost as bad since the two of them yakked to each other the entire trip and totally ignored him. They then argued over directions and led him miles out of the way.

TIP
Buy mosquito repellent before you leave.

TIP
If you elect to drive yourself, obtain a road map before you leave and determine the best route. Your girlfriend will probably only know the way the bus goes. Unfortunately, the bus does not necessarily take the most direct route. It may go through every population centre, every one-horse town and every back street to get there. Unless you want to see a lot of

magnificent countryside, work out the best route before leaving Pattaya. When you get near her village or town, your girlfriend can take over with directions to her home.

The negative reassessment of your disposable cash begins before you leave. Your little darling cannot possibly return to her home with the same 'rags' and borrowed clothing she has been wearing around town. A new wardrobe - or at least a few new dresses - are required so that Mama will be impressed by her daughter's rise up the social ladder on the back of your Visa card. Her village must also see physical evidence that *Lek* has found a kind and generous *farang*. You will therefore also be required to bring 'gifts' for her friends and family. This usually means clothing and food, so you would be advised to do the shopping at a Thai market before leaving.

Being a fair-minded sort of chap, he thought, "OK. I will be eating at their home, so bringing some rice, chilli and other foodstuffs is the least I can do." Wrong! His girlfriend did the shopping alone and they arrived with a 40kg sack of rice, the largest bag of dried chilli ever seen, half a pig and enough green vegetables to feed the entire population of a small country. Oh, and yes, beer - two dozen large bottles.

Upon arrival at the home, be prepared that it may be primitive by Western standards. The house or group of houses will, however, be clean and tidy. Remove your shoes before entering any Thai house.

In Western societies, when a guest is taken to meet the family, he is usually introduced to everyone present. In her village however, do not be surprised if this does not happen. You could possibly only be introduced to Mama and Papa. By this time you should at least know how to say "*sa-wut dee krup*" and to '*wai*' so, if you are introduced to her parents, this is one occasion it would be polite to '*wai*' first, even if you are older than them.

Once you have done this you will probably be left to your own devices due to the fact Thai people are naturally shy around strangers. To be fair, apart from your girlfriend and maybe some of the school children, not many people in her village will speak a word of English. You will be offered a seat, some refreshments and then your girlfriend and her family will catch up on all the gossip - for hours. Do not expect your girlfriend to do any translating for you either.

MONEY NUMBER ONE

This is definitely NOT the way to impress the in-laws!

NEIL HUTCHISON

You will be offered food and it would be bad manners to refuse. Saying that you are not hungry (even if it is true) won't cut it either. Try everything offered to you, even if it is only one mouthful and learn to say "*a-loi*" [delicious]. However, do not drink the water. This is where the beer you should have purchased earlier comes in handy. An added bonus is that beer speaks a universal language and provides an opportunity for you to interact with her male friends and relatives. To them, drinking with you will be akin to reading poetry - free verse.

If you are not already comfortable using a Thai-style toilet, then get used to it pretty quick. Even if the bathroom has a Western pedestal installed, it will probably have a manual flushing system comprising a bucket of water and a plastic ladle. Toilet paper is sometimes not provided so, if that is your requirement, make sure to bring your own. The shower facilities will often be a large water container with ladle and, if you are not used to showering under cold water, get used to that as well.

When the sun starts to go down, it is time to reach for the mosquito repellent. Thai mosquitoes are ferocious, clever and hungry for *farang* blood. Drown your body in repellent. Mosquito coils have limited success and mosquito nets represent only a minor obstacle to the bloodthirsty little devils.

During your visit you may have to refrain from cuddling and kissing your girlfriend in front of other people, although holding hands should not be a problem. Traditional Thais (not so much those you have met in Pattaya or Bangkok) frown on public displays of affection between unmarried couples. If you wish to know more about this, read one of the previously suggested books on the subject of Thai etiquette. Let your girlfriend take the lead. She will not do anything to offend her family so follow her direction.

Just as the Romans would bring their captives home to Rome and parade them through the streets for all to see, your lovely lady will probably take you to meet everyone. She will show you the family estate and be proud to show you off to everyone she knows. And you won't go alone. If you have a hired car, it will always be packed to capacity.

Be prepared. Wherever you go and whatever you do, your lady will want (or expect) you to pay for everything and everybody. This is her way of gaining approval for her choice of boyfriend. Some foreign men have reported they were treated like kings and not allowed to pay for anything during their visit to her home. Certainly this does happen but the family was probably more affluent than most.

MONEY NUMBER ONE

As well as that, during your short stay her friends and relatives will come out of the woodwork with an abundance of imaginative financial woes - told quietly to her for translation before being passed on to you.

Before leaving the nest there is one final duty to perform. You will be required to leave a gift for Mama. This time it is money. If you ask your girlfriend "How much should I give?", she will invariably say "Up to you". This is a trick answer. If you leave too little, your girlfriend will lose face in front of her family. If you leave too much, it becomes a precedent and leaving anything less the next time you visit will be greeted less favourably. The only guide is that 1,000 *baht* is not going to be enough. Don't worry too much, because your girlfriend will respond to your laughably inadequate initial offer by amending it upward to a more respectable figure anyway.

All in all, your trip upcountry will be enjoyable and necessary if you plan to stay with your girlfriend long-term. You will be treated well by her family and friends and get to see some of the 'real' Thailand. And the bonus is you will have some stories to tell your friends back home or in Pattaya. Don't worry - expats are very sympathetic to such tales because every one of them has been through a similar experience at least once.

When Her Relatives Visit You

If Mohammed doesn't come to the mountain then, sooner or later, the mountain will come to Mohammed. Once you have set up a little love nest for yourself and the apple of your loins, you may find one or more of her relatives pay you a visit. With no room at the Inn or the YMCA, the Village People will opt to stay with you. Usually it will be her child or children who come knocking, closely followed by Mama, Papa, sisters, brothers, distant cousins, old school friends etc.

Their visit will be preceded by lots of extra TLC from your darling to help you adjust to what is essentially a *fait accompli*. You're a kind-hearted guy and, what the hell, it's only for a couple of days, right?

Bite the bullet and think about the situation very carefully. No matter how bad it may make you feel and no matter how many arguments may result, you are far better off saying no to the visit than enduring the horrors that can be wrought by a culture clash with your newly-acquired in-laws. They have been known to cause a bigger rift in a perfectly happy relationship than an Exocet missile. To be fair, consider the pros and cons:

NEIL HUTCHISON

The Cons

1. You really don't know how many relatives are going to show up at your door. "Sister me come visit," may mean her sister, sister's husband and five ankle-biters. As a rule of thumb, the number of visitors quoted by your girlfriend is the minimum number. The maximum is the population of her village.

   She told him her family were coming for a short visit. They arrived in two baht buses and he watched as they streamed through his front door. He quickly packed an overnight bag and told his girlfriend he was going to stay at a hotel and to call him when they left.

2. As the host, it will be most polite of you to pay for everything during their stay. As well as providing all-expenses-paid nights on the town, you will pay for all food, all gifts and all transport including their trip home. By that time, you might gladly pay it.

   The love of his life went home for a couple of days and returned with her daughter and sister. He was told only the daughter was coming. On the second day, while out sightseeing, daughter spots a large stuffed doll on a hawker's van. She likes. She wants. His negative response was greeted with daggers from his hitherto affectionate girlfriend. "Why you not buy for she? She like. You no love she? You no love me?" Total fury.
   "No, I'm not going to buy the ungrateful little brat an overpriced toy that I will get no thanks for and she'll destroy in five minutes."
   This, naturally, when translated into Thai, came out as "Of course, my darling, how stupid of me. I love your daughter as if she were my own and her wish is my command." Daughter happy. Girlfriend happy. Don't mention it.

3. Once again, you will receive little or no public displays of affection from your sweetheart for the duration of the stay. As for sex, it is out of the question. You will be lucky if you retain your bed. If Mama comes, you won't.

MONEY NUMBER ONE

"Tee ruk! Mama's here"

4   Your property will be treated as communal property. Before they arrived, what was yours was hers. Now that they are here, what is yours is theirs. Mama may do a mental calculation of the value of all your assets. If she finds something she likes, it will be suggested to your girlfriend that she bring it with her the next time she goes home. All your shampoo, toothpaste and other toiletries will be used up like there is no tomorrow and if they happen to break something of yours, it will be laughed off. "You *farang*. You can buy one more."

5   You will receive no thanks for whatever you do.

The Pros

There are none.

11
Marriage-minded

"The ultimate result of shielding men from the effects of folly is to fill the world with fools."
Herbert Spencer (1820-1903), English philosopher.

A man doesn't have to be in the final stages of brain deterioration due to years of alcohol abuse to consider marriage, but it helps. He is at a distinct disadvantage if he cannot read minds, because the chasm between her intention and his comprehension makes the Grand Canyon look like a bee's navel. That applies to women in general but for a Western male considering marriage to a Thai female, the Canyon gets wider.

In spite of popular opinion and what some 'Introduction Agencies' may tell you, there are very few ladies in Thailand just sitting around waiting to marry a foreigner. A man believing he can simply fly into the country, flash his pearly-whites and run to the altar is barking up the wrong tree. Remember, her first priority is to provide financially for herself and her family. If she believes this can be achieved by marrying a foreigner, then she will consider it. In truth, in spite of what the Bar Hostesses may tell you about not liking Thai men, most would rather marry a Thai with whom they have more in common.

NEIL HUTCHISON

Thai men, in general, have a poor reputation among the Bar Hostesses when it comes to making ideal partners. So why would a Bar Hostess prefer to marry someone like that instead of a kind and generous foreigner? Apart from the Thai man having the same language, culture and interests, the girls like consistency. They know from experience or have heard from friends that a Thai husband may consistently get drunk, consistently cheat on them and consistently resort to violence in marital disputes. Mothers teach their daughters how to address these problems or, at least, how to cope with them.

Foreign men, on the other hand, are a complete mystery to the average Bar Hostess. Apart from the obvious language and cultural differences, she has no idea what to expect from a *farang* husband. This is enough to scare the living hell out of her and propel her to a life that, as bad as it may be, at least she can understand. For those men intent upon marrying a lovely Bar Hostess, overlooking her past and current career choice is only the beginning. Again referring to the novel *Bangkok 8* by John Burdett, the following quote is priceless:

"Prostitution ages women in ways they don't notice at the time. It's not the act of sex, of course, which is perfectly natural and good exercise, it's the emotional stress of continual deception. After all, the customer is only kidding one person that there is any meaning at all in what he is doing: himself. But the girl has to keep up the pretence with one or more men each night. Such stress works the facial muscles, tightening them, producing that hard look prostitutes are famous for, but more important than that, a great dam of resentment builds up in her mind. The first thing a prostitute does when she finds a man willing to look after her is to give up the sex goddess role and probably the charm too. Invariably, she makes the mistake of assuming the customer wanted to marry the real her, not the fantasy, despite the fact that he is only familiar with the fantasy. Then there is a dramatic change in appearance. Many of the girls use hormones to enhance their breasts. Also, there's not a whore in Bangkok who doesn't walk around in six-inch platform shoes. The return to reality can come as quite a shock: from tall, bosomy porn star to flat-chested dwarf. No, prostitutes do not make great wives as a rule, but it has nothing to do with fidelity. Usually the last thing such girls want is an extramarital affair, in which they would probably be expected to play the sex goddess all over again. What they want is the right to be irritable and charmless, which they lost the moment they started on the game."

MONEY NUMBER ONE

In many cases, Thai Bar Hostesses appear so gentle, accommodating, loving, caring, doting, subservient and so willing to please that a foreign man could be excused for thinking he has died and gone to heaven.

At meals, his Thai girlfriend would painstakingly remove all the bones from the fish, even the small ones, before serving it to him. She would also taste the food to make sure it was OK for him. His farang ex-wife, on the other hand, used to just throw him a dead fish and squawk "Cook it yourself!"

But appearances can be deceiving. In part of a letter sent to the Stickman website (www.stickmanweekly.com), a Thai female wrote:

"You give us too much leeway for being Thai. I think this is the biggest mistake you make. You try to understand us with your Western mentality, and when you don't, you think, 'This must be a Thai thing'. It's NOT. Take the money issue for instance. Supporting her whole family is out of the question. It's NOT in the Thai culture that I know. It's a national scam. These poor families are taking advantage of you. It'd be nice of you to help them if you are genuinely inclined to, but the idea of expecting someone who marries into the family to feed the whole extended family is appalling. Don't help us make it a new culture here. Everyone works. Period."

Before doing anything stupid, re-read the list of the Thai Bar Hostess's order of importance in Chapter 6. Have it tattooed on a prominent part of your anatomy, because your position on this list WILL NEVER CHANGE. You are at Number 13 now and no wedding ring, certificate or ceremony will move you up a single notch.

Also take some time to talk to expats. The horror stories related by *farang* who have previously attempted this insanity would fill enough volumes to make Encyclopedia Britannica look like a post card. The true success stories could be carved on the back of a postage stamp with an axe.

NEIL HUTCHISON

A   *An Englishman, close to retirement age, fell in love in Pattaya. He and his girlfriend decided to marry when he retired, at which time he would come to live with her in Thailand. For five years he spent every holiday with her and, when back at work, he sent money to support her. He saved and planned everything, including liquidating all his assets just before he retired so that he could settle down in Thailand with the love of his life. A few days before he caught the plane to Bangkok for the last time, he inexplicably transferred all his money into his intended's bank account in Thailand. When he arrived, guess what? Her bank account was empty and his money and his future wife were gone - never to be seen again.*

B   *A farang fell in love with the most beautiful Thai girl you could ever hope to see. For years he provided her with everything she wanted - money, car, house - and even started a business for her to manage. One day, with no prior warning and no reason forthcoming, she announced that she was getting back together with her farang ex-boyfriend.*

C   *An Englishman married a Bar Hostess from Pattaya. They moved to the UK and lived together for five years. Each year they made several trips back to Thailand for holidays and all appeared rosy. One day, after receiving a phone call from Thailand, the lady told him that she had to go home. He replied that, if she waited a couple of weeks, they could go together. She then dropped the bombshell by telling him that she had to leave immediately because her 'husband' had called to tell her she could come home now. It turned out that she was already married to a Thai man when she married him. The money he had been sending home to her family actually went to her 'real' husband to enable him to build a house and set up a business. When the house was finished, he called to tell her to come home. Her job was done.*

D   *With the wedding planned for next year, the farang bought a house for himself and his Thai fiancée. Since foreigners cannot own land in Thailand, he bought it in his lady's name, filled it with furniture and all was well. On his return from a seven-*

167

MONEY NUMBER ONE

day business trip, he was surprised to find that his key did not fit the lock on the front door. He knocked on the door and was even more surprised when a stranger answered the door. "Who are you and what are you doing in my house?" he asked.

"Your house?" came the reply. "This is my house. I only just bought it!"

Further investigation revealed that, while he was away, the little woman had been very busy indeed. She sold the house, all his furniture and was never seen again.

E *An American fell in love in Pattaya. He was not a poor man, and he and his girlfriend decided to marry. While he was in Pattaya, she stayed with him at his hotel. When he was away, he sent money to support her. One day he arranged to meet her at a restaurant. When she did not show up at the appointed time, he decided to go back to his hotel. Opening the door to his room, he was shocked to find his fiancee in bed with another farang. Apparently, she had met this other guy at a bar and went 'short-time' with him for 500 baht. She even used her fiancee's hotel room. Needless to say, the unamused American threw them both out.*

A *farang*, on hearing that last story, would shake his head in disbelief at the girl's lack of forethought, throwing away what may have been a bright future for a lousy 500 *baht*. Pattaya Bar Hostesses stand there with puzzled looks on their faces as if to say, "So? What is the point of your story?" To them, the girl's behaviour was perfectly understandable.

Ladies working the bar of Pattaya represent only a miniscule fraction of a percent of the female population of Thailand. In expat circles there is continual debate as to whether it is better to seek out a 'decent' lady in preference to one who has spent time working in a bar. In my opinion, the jury will always be out and a definitive answer will probably not be found in my lifetime. In all honesty, I don't consider the Bar Hostesses to be 'indecent' anyway, so the argument is a moot point as far as I am concerned.

The following is a letter from an un-named Thai woman to all *farang* which was posted on a newspaper open forum in April, 2006. There is no way to confirm it but I have no reason to doubt it was, in fact, written by a Thai lady. With no disrespect to the writer, I have taken the liberty of correcting much of the punctuation and grammar while keeping her original meaning.

NEIL HUTCHISON

"I have spent quite a bit of time reading posts on this forum, especially under the topic of 'getting married in Thailand.'

I am sorry to learn that most of you farangs have had negative experiences with your wives' families in terms of money. Most of you here talk about paying a lot of money to support your in-laws. It sounds very much like they are leeches that constantly ask for every pound or dollar out of your wallets.

I am sorry to learn that Thai women marry you for only money for themselves and their families, and only to elevate themselves socially and financially. Once they get what they want from you, they walk away from you.

It sounds like these Thai women give us a bad name.

I do not deny what I learn from your experiences, but I would like you to please not assume that all Thai women are just like that because we are not.

My impression is that those of you who share your stories here all married to women from villages or rural areas where people are un- or low-educated and very poor. That's why what happened to you happened. She and her family wanted your money. You are viewed as a bucket of gold their daughter just happened to fall into, and they can get as much gold out of the bucket as possible. They do that because they are poor, because they have a golden opportunity, because they can, because you allow them to, and because you love your woman.

I believe that there are a lot of Thai women who never want to take advantage of you financially, me included. I believe there are a lot of Thai women who value love more than money. I am from a very humble background. My family and I never ask for money from my American fiancee. If he wants to help us financially, we appreciate that. If not, we continue living without asking. He asked my dad about the dowry he was supposed to give him. My dad told him he wanted nothing; he did not have me for sale. And let me repeat, my dad is poor and low-educated.

We are a poor family who doesn't have a savings account. All my dad wants from him is his love and respect for me.

Again, I am sorry for your bad experience. But for those who are seeking true love with Thai women, have faith that you will find one who just doesn't only crave for your money. You just have to look carefully. Whether rich or poor, good Thai women still exist.

Thank you for reading until this line. I just felt a need to say something here. I am done now."

MONEY NUMBER ONE

That is one of the most sensible letters I have ever read on the subject, and the reason I included it in this revised edition. Following on from her advice to "look carefully", if you are intent on marrying a Thai lady, whether she worked in a bar or a factory in Bangkok, for your own sake, consider these precautions:

1. Never divulge exactly how much money you have in your bank. Do not tell her the PIN number of your ATM card or the combination to your safe if you have one.
2. You control the money. Explain to her what you can afford each month and give her an allowance out of that. Tell her you will take care of her and her alone and insist that you are not going to be the financial salvation for her family and friends. You will not be financially responsible for their multitude of problems.
3. Learn to speak Thai. Taking Thai lessons from a native Thai speaker is best because it is extremely difficult to pronounce the words correctly unless you actually listen to a Thai person saying them. Most importantly, learn the grammar.

The problem with some Thai/English English/Thai dictionaries is they leave out a lot of Thai words and expressions used every day and include many English words that are never used. When was the last time you used the word 'scurvy' in a sentence? How about 'bloodbath', 'dextral' or 'putsch'? Most people don't even know what those last two mean in English.

4. Seek competent legal advice before putting any property into your future wife's name. There are legal ways to protect yourself and your property. Currently, foreigners can legally buy a condo in their own name.

One guy bought a house in his wife's name while ensuring she signed a 30-year renewable lease agreement on the property. These leases are binding and, drawn up correctly, will hold up in a Thai court. The lease agreement was not between his wife and him but his son who lived back in his home country. That way, his wife could not sell the house without his son's permission and neither she nor her parasitic family would benefit financially from his own death. He made sure they all knew it as well.

5. Make a legal Thai Will and have it registered with your embassy. Prenuptual Agreements made *before* the marriage are legal in Thailand. If you intend to leave your lady money or property, never tell her she will be very rich when you die. Don't be worth more dead than alive because, in this part of the world, it can be arranged.

6. Once married, if you wish to reside in Thailand do not live in Pattaya. This town is shrowded in a veil of evil and given time, everyone - and I mean *everyone* - succumbs to it.

    I know of five marriages which began in Pattaya and have stood the test of time (so far). Four of them have one thing in common: the foreigner and his new wife moved out of Pattaya into the country. For the other one, the couple have had two young children together and the lady is happy being a full-time housewife and mother.

7. Leave Pattaya and find a place far away from her relatives and friends, preferably where she doesn't know anybody. If you don't, the very second it becomes known that *Lek* has married a *farang*, her relatives, as well as every person she has ever said "hello" to in her life will come out of the woodwork to grab some of the action. The pressure on her to solve all their financial problems will be enormous.

8. Foreign men tend to enter relationships in Pattaya with a level of trust higher than it should be. Others fear entering a relationship because they are certain they will be cheated or it will cost them too much money. The trick is to strike a balance. Many men living with or married to an ex-Bar Hostess say the same thing.

"I trust her to a point. I trust her with the TV set or the motorbike but would I trust her with the deeds to my house or my life savings? No way. If she suddenly absconded with the television or motorbike, I would get over it and be glad to see the back of her. If she threw me out of the house I bought in her name or she walked off with all my money, I would never recover."

MONEY NUMBER ONE

12
Farang Businessmen

VENI, VIDI, VELCRO!
(I came, I saw, I stuck around!)

*(A parody of VENI, VIDI, VICI – the Latin sentence spoken
by Julius Caesar in 47BC after the Battle of Zela
which is in modern day Turkey)*

Thailand is so wonderful, isn't it? The climate, the food, the smiling people, the lifestyle? And Pattaya? Well, it is just the icing on the cake. Wouldn't it be nice to settle down here and live out the rest of your life in this paradise on earth? You could retire here without too much problem but it would be even better to start your own business and make enough money to keep you in a lifestyle to which you would love to be accustomed. It would also give you something to do in your twilight years. Right?

Maybe, but this chapter is not about showing you how to set up a business in Thailand. There are some very professional books and websites about doing business in Thailand which cover a vast array of legalities and strategies. This chapter is about some of the pitfalls you may encounter. Suffice to say:

*"The only way to make a small fortune in
Pattaya is to start with a large one!"*

Excluding those foreigners who work for large established companies or those on salaries from foreign companies, there are three types of *farang* businessmen in Pattaya.

Type 1: The very small percentage of the working (legally or otherwise) expat population who actually do make money. Not a lot of money, mind you, but enough to make their lives comfortable. These guys rarely become millionaires in dollar terms and are easily recognizable by their flat foreheads caused by continually beating their heads against Thai brick walls. They have thrown away their economics and business management books and theories which work perfectly well in the outside world. They understand the 'Thai way' in their business dealings and decisions and are resolved to playing the Thai game.

Type 2: The ones who don't make much money from their business but simply survive. They invariably have a pension or other source of income coming in from their own country and most of their disposable income is consumed by alcohol. These guys may or may not recognize the 'Thai way' just as they may or may not recognize their own mother. Consciously or unconsciously, they play the Thai game and make up about one quarter of Pattaya's foreign businessmen.

Type 3: The vast majority of the men who come to Thailand, invest in, start up or buy a business venture that devours all their cash reserves within six months. These guys try to run the business the way they would run it in their own country or worse still, let someone else run it while they are out cavorting and drinking what they believe to be the profits. Like a mouse on a treadmill, expending a lot of energy but getting absolutely nowhere, they only last as long as their own money does and walk (or run) away scratching their heads wondering where it all went.

MONEY NUMBER ONE

Dave invested some 50,000 baht in his girlfriend's prawn farm. One day, while drinking with a group of friends, he produced a plate containing some large yet unspectacular prawns for the group.

"Is this a sample of your prawn harvest?" one of the friends asked.

"What sample?" Dave replied sheepishly. "This is it – the entire crop!"

It seems that Dave had failed to take into account certain factors when it came to his business venture. After allowing for all the stock that was stolen from the unguarded pond, all the ones eaten by his girlfriend's family, all of those sold prematurely by these same in-laws and all the prawns that simply died of neglect, his part of the deal amounted to about 500 grams.

"Dave, this is the first time in my life that I've eaten prawns that cost 100,000 baht per kilo."

Dave, of course, failed to see the funny side of it.

Additional factors need to be taken into account when doing business in Southeast Asia - a conglomeration of frustrations which, like ants at a picnic table, come out of nowhere, annoy the living hell out of you, devour all they can and refuse to go away until you have nothing left. Then they leave as quickly and as stealthily as they arrived.

These factors include: people not turning up for appointments; not being able to obtain the simplest piece of information; delays in work for no apparent reason; sudden price rises above the original quote for the job; un-notified law changes; staff not turning up for work; agents running away with deposits; miles of red tape and regulations; extra 'tea money' required if you want the business operating this century; shoddy workmanship etc. The list goes on.

Just like the ants, there is no singular defence, global weapon nor inoculation against them. As soon as you defeat one, another will pop up out of nowhere to take its place. It is a war of attrition. He who is the strongest and can last the longest, wins.

Many bar owners and business people have offered some advice and tips which should be passed on to anyone almost thinking about wishing to investigate the possibility of perhaps conducting a business in Thailand. What follows is a brief summary of opinions from *farang* who have been-there-done-that. The list is just the tip of the iceberg.

NEIL HUTCHISON

1. Never rush into any business deal no matter how great it may sound. Never pay any money up front. Take a lot of time to gather all the information before investing money in any business. Make a list of all the possible scams and ways that you could be cheated out of your investment. Once you have finished the list, remind yourself that the person proposing the deal to you has probably also thought of them – and then some. Nothing is beyond the realms of possibility.

2. Never part with one *baht* or sign any document before obtaining the services of a reputable lawyer. If you don't know one, ask every expat you meet if they can recommend somebody. Attend expat association meetings. Eventually one name will keep recurring, in which case you can be reasonably sure that he or she has at least done the right thing by some expats in the past.

3. Walk, no RUN away from any deal where the other party suggests that you need not go through a lawyer because it will only cost extra money. The same goes if the other party offers the services of his or her own lawyer at a discount price.

4. As a foreigner, you should not attempt to do it on your own. You can have all the great ideas and innovations you like but you need an intelligent Thai partner you can trust to make them legal and put them into effect. Finding the right partner is extremely difficult but your business may fail without him or her. The exact partnership arrangement can be worked out between yourselves. Remember though, your Thai partner will have to be the front man or woman in the business while you keep a low profile.

5. Have all important documents translated into English by an independent source. Better still, obtain two separate translations and compare them to ensure that the meaning is the same.

One poor fellow paid over a lot of cash to buy a boat only to discover later that the ownership transfer document (all in Thai) he signed was for a car, not the boat. He had purchased a very expensive, early model, petrol-guzzling, smoke-belching, rust-bucket of a car and had no way out because he had signed a legal document.

MONEY NUMBER ONE

6   If, at any time during negotiations, you think you smell a rat, be certain it is the biggest mother of a rodent you've ever seen.

7   Apart from your Thai business partner, the less people involved in the management side of the business the better. Try to avoid being talked into hiring or using any friends or relatives of your girlfriend or partner. Never let your wife or girlfriend convince you to use a member of her family as your consultant. "Brother me big lawyer Bangkok. He do for free." He may in fact be a good lawyer and he may also offer his services for free, but who's interests do you think he will be looking after? If you answered, "Mine, because I am his client," go straight to the bottom of the class. Better still, go home, go directly to the airport, do not pass *go-hok* and do not collect 200.

8   Do not count on any help from other people, apart from your business partner, to make your venture a success. It is a sad fact that most of them do not want you to succeed. They want you to fail and the sooner the better. Take, for example, operating a bar. The investor buys the business and pays out a lot of non-refundable money, including 'Key Money'. He may also renovate and upgrade the premises. If the enterprise goes to the wall within a few months, most foreign investors simply walk away. The owner of the premises or the person who owns the lease is then free to sell it again to someone else. He knows that "there is a sucker born every minute." The rent he receives from a working bar is nothing compared to the money he can make by selling it over and over again.

Note: Whenever leasing premises for business purposes, apart from the monthly rent there is often an annual cash fee called 'Key Money' payable to the owner of the lease. The main reason is that the rent is taxable but the annual 'Key Money' is not recorded for tax purposes. Let's say the owner wants to lease the place for 30,000 baht per month. He may instead rent it for 20,000 baht per month plus 120,000 baht 'Key Money'. The other reason is that 'Key Money' is almost always non-refundable.

9   As far as practicable, avoid using agents or intermediaries where money is concerned. Whenever large amounts of cash are transferred or withdrawn, insist that all partners be present at the bank. As happens in many places throughout the world, agents have been known to pocket the money for themselves. When the real owner discovers he has not been paid, the agent is nowhere to be found and receipt or no receipt, the buyer may be required to pay the money again.

10 Use your head at all times and don't let emotion enter into any decision-making. If your ladylove nags you or threatens to leave you if you don't buy this or invest in that, then bid her farewell. It is far better to wave her goodbye than to chance waving goodbye to your money. If the latter did happen, you can be certain that she would follow soon after anyway. Console yourself with the fact that, given the option of losing the love of your life or your life savings, you have lost the one that is the most easily replaced.

11 If you are considering purchasing property, any property, whether it be a condo, shop, bar, house or vacant land, make sure you first find out who actually owns it. This could be difficult as title searches are not as straightforward as they are in the West. The property could be owned by one person, a company, a family or several people. There are also fake or forged titles around. One of the most costly scams involving an unwary *farang* is to sell him property that is not owned or fully owned by the seller. The seller pockets the money and when the real owner or other owner finds out, the authorities can evict the *farang*. Any piece of paper or so-called legal document that the foreigner holds as proof of purchase is not worth the paper it is written on. Sometimes, the real owner or other owners are involved in the scam and the one property can be 'sold' over and over again.

12 This is Thailand. Don't start whinging when things don't go the way you planned. Don't complain that, "back home we do it like this" or "in my country it works like this." You are not in 'your country' so you have to accept the way and the pace at which things are done here.

MONEY NUMBER ONE

13   Follow the example of the Chinese. Ask a Chinese businessman how his business is going and he will complain that he is losing money every day. "Business no good. Only make enough money to eat rice." That is why Hong Kong, Singapore and Taiwan are poor impoverished places, because all Chinese-run businesses lose money. Learn the lesson from the Chinese. If your enterprise is successful and does make money, don't brag about it!

14   There are strict rules regarding foreigners working in Thailand. You are not allowed to work without a work permit and these take effort and money to obtain. You will NOT get a work permit for running a bar. If you own a bar or restaurant and so much as put a glass in the sink, it could be construed as 'working' and you can be deported for it. (Now do you understand Point 14 above? Should you be seen as making a lot of money from your business, one phone call from a greedy friend or jealous competitor can get you into trouble with the authorities.)

A farang invested 4.2 million baht in a Thai owned and operated business (not a bar). He then returned to his home country to obtain the necessary business visa with a view to applying for a work permit once he was back in Thailand. While he was away, his 'business partner' reported him to authorities for working without a permit. Now the farang was stuck in his own country, too scared to return for fear of being arrested at the airport and his partner received a donation of 4.2 million baht.

15   You must be prepared to keep constant control and sight on the daily operation of your business. Don't turn your back on it for a moment and continually check on the cash. Don't let too much cash end up in one person's hands, except yours, of course. Reconcile your financial dealings frequently and personally oversee all work. Don't go on too many 'holidays' and for most of the time, stay sober.

16   Do not listen to any person who tells you they can help you with something because they have one or two powerful friends. "I know big Mafia" or "I am friends with the Chief of Police." Many people exaggerate their sphere of influence in order to elevate their self-

importance. DO NOT rely on any of them to get you out of a jam and it doesn't matter who they say they know or who they are related to. If you ever find yourself in trouble, the only thing that *may* get you out of it is money.

17   As mentioned in the previous chapter on Marriage, NEVER tell your business partner that you have a life insurance policy to provide for them or the business should something unfortunate happen to you. Once again, never be worth more dead than alive.

18   If your business partner also happens to be your girlfriend or wife, don't get caught screwing around. This is especially true if you are thinking about owning or managing a bar. Pattaya is full of temptations but it is a deceptively small place, gossip is the local pastime and YOU WILL GET CAUGHT! As well as probably ending your relationship, it could also end your business. Should there be a non-amicable parting of the ways, guess how much of the business you will end up with?

19   Always remember that this is Thailand. The Western-style legal system doesn't apply here, Western-style business ethics can not be found here and Western-style legal recourse in the case of dishonest business practice is rare.

Does all that scare you? Good.

MONEY NUMBER ONE

13
Conclusion

NEIL HUTCHISON

Love it or hate it, Pattaya is one of the most interesting places in the world. Unfortunately, there are some do-gooders and meddlers of all nationalities who seem determined to change Pattaya. My question to them is: change it into what? If you take away the bars and the girls, what are you going to replace them with? Tear down the bars and replace them with shopping malls? More importantly, what are you going to offer the thousands of people who depend, directly or indirectly, on the income they generate? If the bars closed and the girls left, thousands of Thais would lose their jobs - motorcycle taxi and *baht* bus drivers, hotel staff, food and street vendors, market sellers, beauty salon employees, waitresses and restaurateurs. These people all need to make a living and there is already an oversupply of unskilled labourers seeking jobs. Are the moralists going to offer these people a new 'career' working in a t-shirt factory for 4,000 *baht* per month? There is an old expression that "talk's cheap; whiskey costs money", and not one of the meddlers has yet come up with a viable, economic alternative.

Then there are those Thais who have invested billions of *baht* in plush hotels and local businesses, all of which would face financial ruin should the tourism industry collapse. Some years ago in the Philippines, the pious and infamous Filipino politician, Mayor Lim, closed down every girlie bar in the Ermita district of Manila overnight and turned that once vibrant tourist destination into a dark, dirty and dangerous slum. A similar tactic here would devistate the tourist industry and the local Thai people would ultimately suffer.

Tourists who seek a 'wholesome family' vacation already have plenty of options in Thailand. Places like Phuket and Koh Samui have much better beaches, and Chiang Mai has much better scenery. Pattaya is popular and successful because it is what it is. To change it would be tantamount to killing the tourism golden goose.

Finally, there is the millions of *baht* being sent home (not only by the Bar Hostesses) to families in poor, rural villages each week. Should a girl lose her bar job in Pattaya and be forced to move back home, not only is her entire family deprived of a share of the income she previously made, but now they have another mouth to feed. Are the moralists going to subsidise those families? Are they going to put their money where their big mouths are? Not a chance.

While it lasts, there is no trick to enjoying and loving Pattaya; that part is easy. One group of rabid golfers came here for a seven-day golfing holiday but never touched a golf club or saw a fairway the entire time.

MONEY NUMBER ONE

Another guy extended his visa twice and changed his plane ticket six times because he just could not bear to leave. The trick, therefore, is not to love it too much. To do this you must always remember that it is only a fantasy, a dream. And it is a place where, as one wit noted, "some days you are the bug; some days you are the windshield." So keep your guard up, prepare for the unexpected and have the time of your life while you're doing it. For as complicated, illogical, incomprehensible and as downright irritating as it can be at times, one thing is sure and certain - life here is never dull.

Although I have expressed some sincere personal opinions within these pages, this book was not designed to be a contemporary social commentary nor is it expected to be taken too seriously. It is primarily about fun and laughter but, if it saves only one reader some money or helps him avoid getting into trouble, that is a bonus.

The Go Go dancer told me she had not been at work for a week because a customer had bar fined her for five days. She went on to say that when they parted company at the airport, the farang paid her 100,000 baht. Shocked, I replied that she had indeed had 'chok dee' [good luck]. She leaned towards me, shook her head and smiled, "No. He just stupid!"

There are other topics which could have been covered, some which perhaps should have been covered and more I would have liked to cover. Some, especially regarding legal matters or visa/immigration laws, were deliberately avoided because situations change too quickly. What is the law today may be outdated tomorrow.

The phrase "Money Number One" is the personification of Pattaya but whether you are a millionaire or a pauper, the fun is here to be shared by all. For visitors who have never been to Pattaya before, I will leave you with the words of the toilet-wall philosopher who wrote:

"Don't worry. It only seems kinky the first time."

Some Readers' Comments

"I am writing in appreciation of your extremely informative and amusing tome *Money Number One*. A must read for all would be 'Bar Researchers'. This is my second visit to Pattaya (and not my last I hasten to add) and have benefited from the sound advise within the book." .... Gezza (UK)

"If I only remember part of your comments I will always agree when people say there must be something you don't like about Thailand. I will remember to say, 'Don Muang Airport Departure lounge.'"
.... Tom (UK)

"What a great book! So true! I would like to get a copy for my friends. Is that possible here in the U.S.? I am reading it a second time! I LOVE IT!"
.... Tommy (USA)

"You don't know what great pleasure and a good laugh your book gave me. You wrote all the things I have been thinking for years and you did it in an informative but lighthearted fashion. I have been telling all my friends about it. Good stuff and a great work of literature!!!!"
.... Dave (Nationality Unknown)

"Mate, I could not put the book down until I finished it. All your comments are so true. I could not stop laughing especially how we as *Fa-rungs* rate No 13 on the list. How can we get more copies of your book as I have a number of guys here that need it URGENTLY before they go to Pattaya …" .... Paul (Aus)

"I was just in Pattaya and would have a lot more fun if I had read your book before I got there." .... Troy (USA)

"I enjoyed your book very much. Having lived in and around Pattaya for 10 years I can testify to the accuracy of most of what you say."
.... Ryan (UK)
"Just read your book, couldn't put it down! Every word is so well observed, absolutely spot-on and accurate. I enjoyed reading it and thank you."
.... Greg (UK)

MONEY NUMBER ONE

"Thank you for your books, they were invaluable on my first trip to Thailand ... the bar girls could not believe it was my first trip, thanks to your books, although I still like to believe they were a tad on the cynical side and I hold a glimmer of hope for finding love in Thailand yet."
.... Mick (Aus)

"I have purchased and read three of your books; *A Fool [in Paradise]*, *The Fool is Back* & *Money Still Number One*. I think that they are a great read and having read them after a couple of trips to Pattaya they are right on the money." .... Rob (Aus)

"My little *teeluk* sat reading Thai comic magazines, occasionally glaring at me and the book I was reading ... every now and then she would make a comment, 'You like book?' to which I replied 'Yes I like book, it all about you.' This gained the response, 'I know, book no good, it good for you, no good for me.'" .... Tony (UK)

"Never have I read true meaning of a book in my life. Everything the girls did and said was in your book. They are the greatest actresses of all time."
. ... Rodney (Aus)

"I had the wonderful experience of reading your lovely book before my first stay in Pattaya, and it provided me with very valuable information and also a very enjoyable reading pleasure." . ... Gerald (Germany)

... and the best for last:

"I have to read your book *Money Number 1*! ... i m thai girl i dont like that you write fucking wrong about thai lady !!!!!! if you think bad to the girls why do you have to fucking come to many time to thai !!!!!??????? i know we are work for fucking buddy but you know we are have to!!!!!!!!!!!!!!!!!!!!!"
.... Name Withheld (Pattaya Bar Hostess)

184

Made in the USA
Las Vegas, NV
04 February 2021